About this Book

What happens when we tap into the wealth within us? As you will see in this uplifting, new work from Charlene Costanzo, ordinary days start to sparkle with extraordinary moments, and all areas of our lives are enriched. In this empowering book, Ms. Costanzo shares real life examples of triumphs, transformations, and healings that result from using our inherent gifts of strength, beauty, courage, compassion, hope, joy, talent, imagination, reverence, wisdom, love, and faith. Each "touchstone" in this collection of stories can inspire us to stay in touch with our inner gifts, even when—especially when—fear, hurt, anger, or doubt has derailed us.

How did *Touchstones: Stories for Living The Twelve Gifts* come to be? In 2000, while promoting her bestselling book, *The Twelve Gifts of Birth,* Charlene traveled America in a motor home. It was then, while visiting schools, shelters, prisons, and places of worship, that Charlene began to watch closely for evidence of The Twelve Gifts in herself and in others. This daily practice became a personal quest, one in which she invites us to join her. The stories within are intended to spark memories, recognitions, and appreciations of times we used our gifts and to ignite enthusiasm for building our own collection of touchstones. Reading *Touchstones* can lead to living The Twelve Gifts more abundantly.

Also by Charlene Costanzo

The Twelve Gifts of Birth
A parenting classic and message for all ages

The Twelve Gifts in Marriage
Wisdom for all states of the relationship

The Twelve Gifts for Healing
For all the times when life hurts

The Thirteenth Gift
A celebration of wonderment

Touchstones

STORIES FOR LIVING THE TWELVE GIFTS

CHARLENE COSTANZO

FEATHERFEW™

FEATHERFEW™

Sedona, Arizona and Winter Garden, Florida

TOUCHSTONES: STORIES FOR LIVING THE TWELVE GIFTS

Text Copyright © 2012 by Charlene Costanzo

Cover design by Karen C. Heard
Text layout and design by 1106 Design
Printed in the United States of America
Distributed by Midwest Trade Books

Publisher's Cataloging-in-Publication
(Provided by Quality Books, Inc.)

Costanzo, Charlene.
    Touchstones : stories for living the twelve gifts /
by Charlene Costanzo.
    p. cm.
    LCCN 2011933793
    ISBN-13: 978-1-891836-01-5 (pbk.)
    ISBN-10: 1-891836-01-3 (pbk.)
    ISBN-13: 978-1-891836-02-2 (ebook)
    ISBN-10: 1-891836-02-1 (ebook)
    1. Self-actualization (Psychology) 2. Conduct of
life.   I. Title.
BF637.S4C67 2011   158.1
                    QBI11-600166
            10 9 8 9 6 5 4 3 2 1

For you

*"At the wondrous moment you were born,
as you took your first breath,
a great celebration was held in the heavens,
and twelve magnificent gifts were granted to you."*
— FROM THE TWELVE GIFTS OF BIRTH

Contents

Contents

Introduction

Dear Reader,

I'd like to tell you how this book got its title, how it came to be, and what I hope for you, as you read it.

Touchstones? What Are They, Exactly?

Before we look into the meaning of "touchstones," let's consider what good companions stones have been on our journey as a species over the last 600,000 years or so. Our great, great, great (and many more greats) grandparents used stones to hunt, gather food, start a fire, cook, build dwellings, make clothing, communicate, record life experiences, and protect themselves. Stones helped our ancestors to survive!

Then, about 700 BC, people began to use a particular kind of stone in a way that helped them to thrive. Someone observed how a distinctive streak was left upon a smooth, black stone when it was "touched" by gold; hence, those stones were called "touchstones."

By carrying a touchstone that held the mark of true gold, people could readily test the authenticity of a piece of gold offered in trade. One would simply stroke the offered gold nugget or trinket upon the stone—making another mark—and compare that mark against the first streak. If the marks matched, the payment offered could be trusted and accepted. As a result of a touchstone's ability to reflect true value in this way, people were able to conduct business more easily. In time, this led to the widespread use of coins, which led further to the building of wealth... *material wealth.*

Over the years, the word "touchstone" has grown beyond that original, very tangible definition and come to mean: *an example of the intangible excellence or genuineness of something.*

I love this evocative word. *Touchstone.* I've come to use it for: *things that reflect the excellence within humanity and the true value in you and in me... our spiritual wealth.*

An Invitation to Mine

Like gold buried in pockets under the surface in our physical world, there is wealth in our core. The wealth in us is in the form of *strength, beauty, courage, compassion, hope, joy, talent, imagination, reverence, wisdom, love, faith,* and other gifts of life.

I believe that the wealth within us is far more powerful than gold. No, not in the world's eyes (at least not yet). We can't use it to buy things. We can't bank it or invest it. However, we can mine "wealth of soul" and use it to enrich every area of our lives—our health, homes, relationships, work, dreams—everything.

Touchstones for The Twelve Gifts

Like those long-ago ancestors who carried physical touchstones, you and I can carry about, in our minds and hearts, touchstones that reflect a streak of *strength, beauty, courage, compassion, hope*—life's gifts. I like to think of these gifts as God's Gold in us.

How This Book Developed

I've been gathering a collection of touchstones for more than ten years now. My touchstones include quotes, affirmations, anecdotes, activities, songs, symbols, films, and fables that demonstrate The Twelve Gifts in action.

Among my most treasured touchstones are true stories.

Consider how we already carry a host of stories within us. All our memories, judgments, conclusions, and beliefs are stories. Everything that we ever experienced—and the way we interpreted what happened—is a story. We already use our personal stories, usually without realizing it, as we act and react during the course of every day.

Some of our stories keep us small, such as the ones that tell us we are unlucky, or clumsy, or stupid, or ugly, or weak, or "not good enough."

On the other hand, we are uplifted, expanded, and empowered when we think positive thoughts and use life-affirming stories to influence our choices.

Even just one touchstone can serve us well. How? For example, when I face a challenge and feel confusion or fear, by holding, in my mind and heart, *Falling into Place,* which is one of my touchstone stories for hope, the hope energy within me resonates and stirs. I begin to trust in what is unfolding. And I genuinely experience hope! Peace often follows, along with a sense of beauty. In that moment I am strengthened. And I'm likely to then be inspired with guidance from the gift of wisdom.

I started collecting touchstone stories while on a book tour for *The Twelve Gifts of Birth.* For one full year, my husband and I traveled throughout the United States in a motor home, visiting schools, shelters, prisons, places of worship, hospitals, and bookstores.

We called that journey "The Polished Stone Tour," in part because everywhere we went, we offered a shiny stone to every person we encountered.

Each polished stone was meant to anchor the message of *The Twelve Gifts of Birth* as it passed on to each opened hand.

The use of stones on that tour, and our naming it "The Polished Stone Tour," were serendipitous. Before the tour, I had used polished stones to encourage some students to believe in their inner beauty and strength. When a third-grade boy wrote, "Thank you for reminding me I'm not a plain old worthless rock. I'm like the shiny stone you gave me. I keep it in my pocket and touch it when I'm scared," I decided to offer the symbolic stones everywhere we went. So, when we moved into our house on wheels, which was jam-packed with all our personal stuff, we made room for thousands of stones.

Into every place I entered (except for prisons, where the stones were not permitted), I carried a hidden fish bowl that was filled with agates, amethysts, apache tears, moonstones, bloodstones, tiger eyes, stones of citrine, aquamarine, lapis, jade, and rose quartz. At the end of each presentation, I reached into my big bag and displayed the bowl. Before giving a stone to each person present, I explained the symbolism of the stones and the reason behind my gesture.

On the top of the pile, there was a rough, unpolished stone. I held that up for all to see. "At times we feel like this stone… plain, ordinary, not valuable, maybe even worthless," I said. "But when stones like this are tumbled and polished, look how beautiful they are inside." And I went on to explain how we are like the shiny stones. Inside, we are all valuable. "So, for those times you feel bad about yourself, hold your stone and remember the beauty and the strength and all the gifts that are inside you."

Isn't it interesting that a rock's inner beauty is revealed through a process of tumbling and the reality of our gifts is brought forth, in part, by the tumbles and stumbles we experience?

A glass bowl filled with a variety of polished stones holds two other symbolic lessons. The first is a reminder that, like the stones, we come in all different shapes, colors, and sizes. And, we are all beautiful. The second is revealed when we take a close look at any one of the stones. Each has a few nicks and scratches. Not one is perfect. Neither are we. Like the stones, we have flaws, wounds, scars— *and* we are beautiful.

As the year passed, many children and adults said that the stone they received became a reminder of their worthiness in times of doubt. And, they gave examples of The Twelve Gifts in action. Every encounter on that journey made a mark on me. Hearing the stories of others led me to reflect more on my own experiences with each of the gifts, in the present and in the past.

My Hopes for You

If we meet in person someday, I'll offer you a polished stone. (I always carry a few.) In the meantime, I offer you this sampling of touchstone stories. For the most part, the stories within this book reflect life's gifts in ordinary situations, not highly dramatic ones. I want to demonstrate how bringing these gifts into our (seemingly) ordinary days can bring more and more moments of wonderment, well-being, and authentic happiness.

Introduction

I hope the stories within this book will touch you, leave a mark, and guide you to better recognize the gold that lies within you. Looking for the gifts has become a daily practice for me, a quest on which I invite you to join me.

I took a physical journey through America. That outward journey led me to a deeper inward one… a kind of pilgrimage.

Life itself is a journey, is it not? "A hero's journey" that each of us is here to make, according to Joseph Campbell.

I hope that, for a little while, you will let this book be like a map on your life journey—or, a companion. Travel through this book in your own chosen way, at a rate that feels comfortable for you. Linger when you feel called to stop and rest. Go slow and savor. Or speed through. It's your journey.

I hope that, along the way, you will gather some of your own familiar-and-favorite touchstones and discover new ones. At the end of each chapter you'll find quotes and questions that are intended to help you do that. After reading this book, you are likely to have your own collection of touchstones. Perhaps you'll want to share a story or two.

I'd love to hear from you! Please write to me at www.charlenecostanzo.com.

Wishing you the best of life's gifts,

Charlene

Strength

*May you remember to call upon
it whenever you need it.*

Mazi and the Little Brown Dog

In Mesa, Arizona, I met a soft-spoken woman named Mazi. "I *know* I have strength," she said. "And I remember the exact date I found this to be true: July 19, 1979." With bright eyes and a broad smile, Mazi seemed to grow taller than her five-foot stature as she shared her story.

On that date over thirty years ago, Mazi was living with her seven-year-old son and her aging mother in Ajmer, a small desert town in northwest India. Many dogs roamed the streets in Ajmer, and that summer Mazi befriended one. Every day a little brown dog came to her home, searching for food and shelter from the hot sun. Mazi looked forward to the visits, especially when she noticed the dog's belly swelling with a litter of puppies.

With the monsoon season approaching, Mazi, like everyone else in Ajmer, prepared for two to three months of intensified rainfall. She had an ample supply of candles and oil lamps, knowing that electricity would often be turned off during the heavy rains. That summer, the rains were torrential. On July 19, when the water reached flood proportions, Mazi, her son, and her mom climbed the stairs of their one-story home to the rooftop. As the sky darkened and the rain poured, they watched as cattle and furniture rushed by in a massive, muddy river.

"Suddenly, I noticed a dog—*that* dog—standing precariously on the wall surrounding our house. It was as if my heart burst open," she said. "I *had* to save her."

Strength emerged in the form of determination, and it rose within Mazi like the water rising around her. Without hesitation, she worked her way down the stairs and through the house. Pushing through chest-high water, hardly able to see in the darkness, Mazi finally reached the front door. There, with a mixture of resolve and physical strength, she forced the door open and pressed on through the floodwater to the wall. Despite the pressure of the water, Mazi stood steadily and lifted the dog from the wall. And then, she turned around and repeated the whole grueling effort, in reverse: back to the door, through the house, and up to the roof, while holding the dog above the water.

"I continue to be amazed at the enormous physical strength *and* strength of purpose that filled me that day," Mazi stressed, "especially since I didn't know how to swim! But, I loved that little dog. I was so afraid she would be swept away before I could reach her! Since then I have known: *I have strength!*"

The Five-Pound Switch

"At the end of 2009, I was at the lowest point of my life," said Heather. "My husband and I had lost our dream home to foreclosure. My income as a realtor had shrunk to almost nothing. On top of that, we had two rental homes that we had to sell—at a loss. I was deeply depressed."

Heather went on to say that, while she had always had an appreciation for white wine, her affection for it was developing into an unhealthy habit.

"It was not unusual for me to polish off a whole bottle in one night," said Heather. "It helped blanket the pain."

In January 2010, Heather heard a sermon that changed her life. The pastor of her church asked the congregation to reflect on their accomplishments during the past decade.

"Other than being a good mom, I felt that I had *no* accomplishments," she said. "In fact, anything and everything I had achieved was lost—our home, our rental properties, my career, and my identity as a successful realtor." Heather shuddered and added, "My sense of pride was gone too. Previously, I had felt that I was helping make dreams come true. But, all those buyers were losing equity! So, instead of pride in what I had done, I felt as if I was partly responsible for other people's hurt."

Pastor Dave then asked everyone to think about what they would like to do in the next decade that would make it better than the last.

Heather pictured her drinking habit. *First, I need to change that*, she thought. *That won't be easy. I doubt I have the will power to stop. I need to get out of my rut. How? What can I do? I'm hurting. I feel helpless.* On and on she thought of how she felt weak and stuck.

The pastor then asked everyone to envision a railroad. He explained that, at each intersection of tracks, there is a switch that controls the train track. That switch weighs only about five pounds.

Yet, with a simple flip of the switch, a train weighing tons and traveling 150 miles per hour can easily go in a different direction.

"I saw that switch in my mind," said Heather. "And I felt the power of a train barreling down the tracks at incredible speed and force. It would be tough to stop that! In fact, isn't there an expression that you *can't* stop a speeding train?"

Even before the pastor drew the analogy, Heather got it. *God can flip that switch in me!*

"I prayed for help with all my heart," she said. "And I felt that it had been done. The switch was flipped. I was headed in a new direction with the strength to go in that direction."

That Sunday was the day that Heather stopped drinking. Since then, the image of the five-pound switch has been Heather's touchstone for strength.

"Sometimes I can hardly believe how far I've traveled since that switch into a new direction," she said. "Not only have I not had a drop of alcohol since then, I wrote and published a book! When the clarity of my mind was no longer dulled by alcohol,

I could better see who I am and what I want to do. I remembered my childhood dream to write, and I had the strength to act on that dream. I now picture that five-pound switch whenever I feel the need for strength to go in a new direction about anything."

Strength Inherited?

Unlike most moms in the early 1950s, mine had an outside job. During the hours my mom worked, I was usually in the care of my paternal grandparents. Often, I would ask them to tell me stories about when they were children.

In my mind's eye, I can still see one particular time at their house. My grandpa, sitting across from me at the kitchen table, is grinding mounds of walnuts for the Christmas nut rolls. Grandma is bustling about between the stove and the sink, cooking and cleaning up.

"Tell me more, Grandma, about the old country. Tell me again, Grandpa, about the pigs."

Like many times before, they happily gave me glimpses of their childhood years in what had been Austria-Hungary. I delighted in picturing my plump, short-haired, graying grandmother as a pretty girl with golden-brown braids and my grandfather as a handsome, industrious young boy.

One thing that helped me to imagine how Grandma looked was the single, long, thick braid of her hair that she had cut as a young woman and kept in a draw-string bag in her nightstand drawer. I loved to touch the actual hair that had been on her head long ago. I associated that braid with the fairy-tale character Rapunzel, and I imagined the "old country" looking like illustrations I saw in my favorite picture books.

Similar to the way I experienced anxiety, sadness, hope, and joy when I listened to all the famous fairy tales, my emotions rode up and down through the tensions and triumphs of my grandparents' real life experiences.

My favorite story was how my grandpa had herded pigs. Yes, pigs. Not sheep. Pigs.

I tried to picture that long-ago time when my grandpa's mother and father—my great grandparents—traveled on a boat from that "old country" to this "new country." With them, on that journey across the vast ocean, they brought *four* of their *six* children. Not *all* of their children! They had left my grandfather, just twelve years old, and his fourteen-year-old brother behind, on the other side of the world! It reminded me of Hansel and Gretel, left alone in the woods!

"How *could* they do that, Grandpa?! Didn't they love you?" I asked.

It took many times of my grandfather explaining before I began to accept that his parents did what they had to do to start a new life for the whole family. Until his father and mother got established in America and saved enough money for the remaining two children to join the family, my grandpa and his brother could fend for themselves. It was understood: they *could* fend for themselves.

My grandpa glowed with pride every time he reminisced about how he and his brother slept in barns as they worked from neighboring farm to farm and how they cared for all the pigs in the area. Extended family and friends in the village fed the boys and looked out for them while the brothers waited for passage to the new world. For my grandpa, that time was a grand adventure, during which he and his brother proved their manhood.

As Grandpa continued to grind walnuts, Grandma joined us at the table for more story-telling.

I didn't call it "strength" until years later. But it was clear to me that my grandfather had something powerful in him, something to be admired. My grandmother had it too.

I'm not sure when it was, but I know that there *was* a time when I sat with them at that table, noticed that the color of my eyes matched theirs, and wondered: *Might I have in me what I see in them?*

What I now know—at least it is what I believe with all my heart—is that we all have within us what I saw in my grandparents. And I understand that what I inherited from them was their *valuing* of strength, which helps us to bring it forth.

The One-Word Prayer

During the three years my mother was being treated for leukemia, I traveled often from Arizona to New Jersey to be with her and to help my father with her care. On one such visit, when I finally arrived after several delays and a bumpy flight, I felt drained on all levels.

After depositing my suitcase in my former bedroom and visiting with my parents in their living room, I walked into the kitchen. The first thing I noticed was that the bright yellow ceramic bowl on the kitchen table was empty. Usually it held an assortment of fresh fruit. Then, I opened the refrigerator. It held little to offer. The entire kitchen seemed to reflect how I felt—empty.

The emptiness of the fruit bowl and the refrigerator—the absence of my mom's touch and energy in the kitchen—triggered a flood of painful emotions in me. Instead of feeling empty, in that instant I felt saturated with resistance to what was happening around me and within me. Suddenly, I wanted to open the kitchen door that led to the yard and run. And run. And run some more. Run until I released all the overwhelming fear, anger, and sadness.

Instead, I stood still, closed my eyes, slowly inhaled, and whispered, *Strength.* Literally, I called for it. And with grace, it came, immediately and with a force so full that it startled me.

If you were to ask me to describe what that was like, I would ask if you ever watched a Popeye cartoon. Similar to how that character was transformed after eating a can of spinach, ready to take on the world, I felt completely energized—physically, mentally, and emotionally. I was ready to take on everything that was *my* world at the time—which was to shop, cook, clean, and be lovingly present for my parents.

Sometimes, that's all it takes: remembering to call upon it. Just once.

And sometimes we have to call for it, again and again.

Walking the Talk

I n September 2000, I was diagnosed with advanced Non-Hodgkin's Lymphoma and told, "There is no cure." At first I felt frozen with fear, with almost no strength at all. For a few days, I let cancer define me.

Restful sleep came only near dawn, after hours of anguished tossing and turning. I would wake in the new day with a split second of peacefulness and then remember, *Cancer cells have invaded my body, and they are growing.*

I wanted to learn about lymphoma, but I could digest only a little bit of information at a time. It took great strength just to read the material and look at diagrams of aberrant cells. It took tremendous strength to face the reality of my diagnosis.

The disease led me to examine my convictions.

In *The Twelve Gifts of Birth* I had written about strength: *May you remember to call upon it whenever you need it.* I had offered that advice to so many others in both my personal and professional life. *Could I heed it now?* During the previous year on the Polished Stone Tour, I had said to thousands of children and adults throughout the country, "No matter who we are, no matter what we face, we have these powerful gifts within us that can help us heal, enrich, and empower every area of our lives."

Hm-m-m. *Could I walk my talk? Would I?*

Before the first of six chemotherapy treatments, my doctor said, "This is a time to draw upon your strength. It will make a difference. Do what makes you strong."

I gave a lot of thought to that: What makes *me* strong? Dealing with cancer—or any life challenge—can be a means to discovering more inner strength. But how? We all have our own ways of coping and responding. How do I figure out what works best for me? And will I have the strength to do it?

Strength

So, I gave a great deal of thought to the question, *What empowers me?* After praying, reflecting, and tuning in for inner guidance, I recalled a story I had heard in a high school class about Ivan Pavlov. He is most famous for his behavior studies with dogs. But did you know that when Pavlov was ill with a serious infection (before the discovery of penicillin) he did something remarkable to make himself strong?

He played with a bucket of mud. Yes, mud. With his hands in a bucket of mud from a nearby river, Ivan re-enacted a scene from his childhood: in his mind, he saw himself playing in the warm mud next to his mom while she did the laundry in the river. He even envisioned her singing and telling him stories—something she always did. Apparently, the sense of well-being and joy Ivan re-created for himself was so strong that it returned him to homeostasis. Eventually, the fever broke and he was cured.

Remembering this about Ivan Pavlov led me to a variety of activities that were like my own version of "playing in the mud." I never enjoyed playing in the mud as a child. But the sand? Oh yes! I loved making sand castles at the New Jersey shore, swimming in the ocean, and going on boardwalk rides. So, I recreated a sense of my childhood love of the seashore—the joy and well-being that went with that—by smelling suntan lotion every morning.

I also re-enacted other childhood experiences of happiness by dancing, daydreaming, and coloring while listening to soothing music. I blew bubbles, played jacks, and turned a few cartwheels (clumsily, which led me to laugh and lighten up). All these simple activities seemed to fill and re-fill a tank of strength in me, so that an abundant supply of strength was always ready to flow through me.

During the five months of chemotherapy, I needed to call upon that reserve of strength again and again: on treatment days when I welcomed the toxic chemicals into my body, to do their intended work; for the twenty-four hours following each chemo cocktail, when my body felt like a dried-out, hot oven, and I needed strength to accept that sensation; and to embrace being completely hairless and to become comfortable in my body instead of feeling like an alien being. I also needed strength to shift my focus again and again from fear to hope.

It seemed wise to nourish strength daily and keep the supply flowing and growing. I made sure, no matter how tired or listless I may have felt, that I regularly filled my strength tank by engaging in activities that empowered me. In addition to the childhood re-enactments, I drew strength from nature, music, books, films, friends, family, therapeutic touch, aromatherapy, inspirational stories, meditation, and prayer.

My doctor had given me sound advice. He was right. Building strength *did* make a difference... in many ways. Among those ways, after five months of treatments, all tests results said: *No evidence of cancer.*

I continue to let those words guide me: *Do what makes you strong.* It seems to me that, no matter what is going on—in *my* world, or in *the* world—it is always a very good time to magnify and to draw upon strength.

*"When you look back over your life and see
how much you've had to face... it's interesting
to try and pinpoint the first time... you
had to reach inside yourself and pull out
strength you didn't know you had."*

—LORETTA LYNN

If I'm afraid, it doesn't mean that I'm not brave.
And if I doubt, it doesn't mean that I've lost faith.
And if I fall, if doesn't mean I can't go on.
And if I cry, it doesn't mean that I'm not strong.

—JANA STANFIELD AND KAREN TAYLOR-GOOD,
"DOESN'T MEAN THAT I'M NOT STRONG"
FROM THE CD, *BRAVE FAITH*

When you're scared just remember,
Just remember... you are strong.
When you're confused just remember,
Just remember... you are strong.
When you're scared and confused
And you don't know what to do
Just remember to remember you are strong.

—SUSAN KAY WYATT, ROB PETERS, AND KASI PETERS,
"I AM STRONG"
FROM THE CD, *THE TWELVE GIFTS OF BIRTH MUSIC*

For Reflection, Journaling, and Discussion

1. Do you consider yourself to be a "strong" person? Why or why not?

2. How have you used strength? Start by recalling a particular time when you called upon strength. Was it to face a challenge? To complete a project? To follow a dream? To be present in a situation? Remember that strength takes many forms, such as will, resolve, determination, and perseverance; and it can be brought into all aspects of our lives.

3. What stirs a feeling of empowerment in you?

4. From what activities do you draw strength? Praying? Walking? Meditating? Dancing? Swimming? Talking with a friend? Playing rousing music?

5. In what situations and areas of your life would you like more strength to flow?

Beauty

May your deeds reflect its depth.

A Book by Its Cover

O ne day I received a call from a priest who wanted me to read my book and give a presentation to teens living in the residential facility where he worked in Manhattan. I felt honored by his invitation and excited about the opportunity to visit Covenant House.

Two months later, as the autumn sky darkened and I looked for the Upper West Side halfway house, I felt trepidation. I realized that, besides feeling uncomfortable in that particular neighborhood, my ego feared rejection. It seemed unlikely to me that these teens would want to hear a *Once upon a time* fairy tale read by a middle-aged, middle-class woman who knew nothing about the streets. When I found the building, I paused at the door. Asking my ego to step aside, I took a deep breath and entered the facility.

Eight residents showed up for the presentation, seven females and one male. On first impression, they looked stonehearted. Generally the young people staying there had been involved in drugs, prostitution, theft, and other behaviors that don't reflect what society considers "beauty."

Despite their surface appearances, that night, while I read, as arms uncrossed and jaws relaxed, I glimpsed soul beauty emerging through their eyes and softening expressions. They seemed to see it also, in themselves and one another. As time passed, the young women spoke openly. Each had been abused in childhood. Each was trying to heal. They shared longings and dreams for the future.

The lone male, in contrast to the growing chatter and gesturing of the females, remained quiet and motionless in a small chair that emphasized the length of his limbs and brawn of his large, imposing body. Had I encountered him outside the facility, I might have crossed the street to avoid him. When the discussion ended, lingering behind the others, he was the last of the group to approach me to receive my customary gift of a polished stone, symbolizing the value and beauty in each of us. For several moments, after receiving his stone and closing his fist around it, he stood still, towering over me. Silently, he looked directly into my eyes, as tears gathered in his. Gazing back into his glistening eyes, I felt completely free of fear. I saw his humanity. I saw beauty.

Finally, letting tears drop, the formidable young man bent down, hugged me gently, and whispered, "Thank you, lady."

As he then turned away and left quickly, I thought to myself, *And thank you, young man, for this lesson.*

Hidden Cathedrals

My encounter with teens in recovery at Covenant House in New York reminded me of what my husband and I had experienced in Carlsbad, New Mexico, and in Benson, Arizona. In both desert locales, the terrain looks harsh on the surface. Spiky and scrubby vegetation grows through parched, rocky soil on which scorpions creep and rattlesnakes slither. However, *beneath* the landscape in those places, underground, there is nature's version of a grand cathedral.

Carlsbad Caverns in New Mexico and Kartchner Caverns in Arizona are among the world's most significant caves. Just as cathedrals feature magnificent chapels with glorious columns, arches, and artistic creations, caves consist of majestic chambers with gorgeous stalactites, stalagmites, and other spectacular formations. Standing still in one of those golden subterranean rooms, after recovering from numbing awe and gratitude for what I saw and felt, I marveled, "Who would imagine that such stunning beauty is hidden underground? But here it is for all who seek it… or somehow stumble upon it."

Within each of us there is a place like that: sparkling and sacred. Like many of the world's caverns, our beauty may be hidden under rough outer appearances. Yet, it is always there, ready to be discovered.

The Beach Garden

One morning, during a vacation respite in Florida, I walked briskly along the beach on Sanibel Island, a barrier island off the coast of Ft. Myers. Keeping pace with the music playing through my earphones, I stepped carefully around sandcastles and people searching for shells. With a row of dolphins arching just beyond the breaking waves and hundreds of birds nibbling at the shoreline, it was easy to appreciate nature's beauty.

About a half mile into my aerobic walk, I felt drawn to a sand creation beyond the high-tide line. I pulled off the earphones and walked up from the water's edge to get a closer look. A simple, Zen-like garden had been made of leaves, twigs, and shells, some broken and some whole. In front of the garden, seaweed formed the word, *Welcome*.

I wondered if the greeting was intended for beach walkers, for imaginary creatures, or for the waves that would eventually claim the creation. The garden was not nearly as impressive as the sand castles I had passed; however, it exuded beauty nonetheless. In fact, I liked it so much that I decided to take a picture of it. Later when I returned to the beach debris garden with my camera, I met the family who created it. After talking with them I understood why its beauty was so palpable.

The mother explained that she, her husband, and two preteens had made a similar beach-art creation the day before. They'd had fun playing together, she said. When they stepped back and saw the result, they were pleased and hoped that beach walkers would enjoy it.

When they came out to the beach early this next morning, however, they discovered that it had been destroyed. Footprint evidence suggested that someone had stomped through their little creation, deliberately swishing and smashing his large feet around in it.

"When I saw the hurt on my children's faces, intense anger rose in me," said the mother. "Who would do such a thing? Why? I wanted to crush whoever did it."

She went on to say that, fueled by fury, she marched down the beach with fast, fierce steps, cursing the young man she imagined doing it, wishing him harm. She walked until her anger was spent, which brought her to the lighthouse at the end of the island. There she sat and thought. *What are my children learning from this? That some people are senselessly mean? To mistrust? To hate?*

"When I released the last of my anger, I felt something open," she said. "And the Dalai Lama came to mind. A sixth of the Tibetan population was killed in the 1950s. When he is asked about that holocaust, he responds with compassion for the people who did it. I then saw other possible lessons my children could learn from this experience."

When she arrived back at the site, she asked her family to forgive the perpetrator and help her repair the garden. At first they resisted. So, she started to rebuild it herself. Soon, her husband joined her. Then, the daughter. Finally, the son. After a short time, they worked again in a playful way with ease and trust. They enjoyed another morning in the sunshine, arranging flotsam and jetsam in attractive patterns. They forgave the debris garden vandal, wished him (or her) well, and agreed that what emerged this second time around was actually far prettier than what they had made the day before. When it was done, the son suggested adding the word "Welcome" as a greeting *and* an acceptance of whatever would become of it.

Such beauty.

A Kaleidoscope Named Zoey

I love kaleidoscopes. In fact, I've got a collection of them. Ever since I got my first little cardboard one when I was a young child, I've been enthralled with them.

I like to first look directly at the end where the individual pieces of "stuff" are. The "stuff" might be pebbles, seeds, or bits of plastic. My favorite one contains shards of green, blue, and yellow glass. Whatever the contents, the pieces at that end often look ordinary and unimpressive. However, when we lift the cylinder toward the light, look though the window on the other end, and turn the device—*Wow*! Those plain bits of "stuff" transform into delightful patterns of beauty.

Zoey reminds me of my favorite kaleidoscope.

Beauty

Zoey grew up under the strict standards of a strong, controlling father. Not once did he ever tell her she was pretty—not once when she was a little girl, a teenager, or an adult.

Her reserved mother encouraged her to become well-educated and independent; however, her mother didn't help Zoey see beauty in her face, her body, or her actions. And Zoey never did. She remembers that she saw beauty in trees, animals, and clouds—but never in herself. She remembers playing dress-up once, wanting to feel pretty. Instead of being complimented, she was criticized by her father.

Zoey felt that she didn't fit in at school, in part because her wardrobe was hand-made by her mother, who also cut Zoey's hair in a plain, practical style. One school morning during pubescence, when Zoey came to the breakfast table, her father angrily led her to the sink and scrubbed her face. He thought she was wearing makeup. But she wasn't. Her youthful cheeks and lips were just naturally lustrous and pink.

"In countless ways, as I was growing up, I was getting the message that I was ugly," she says. "By the time I reached high school I was overeating to fill feelings of emptiness and depression. I felt broken inside."

Years later, Zoey began to see herself differently. "First, I had to be willing to," she says. "And I work at it, still. I've had thousands of negative messages to replace with positive ones."

During therapy Zoey found and framed a photo of herself when she was four years old. Looking at it, she could see that she had been a bright-eyed, beautiful little girl. That picture, along with affirmations, journaling, and other tools, helped Zoey to overcome feelings of shame and unworthiness. "I had to bring back to life the spirited little girl I once was. Every day for years I spoke heartening words to the little girl in the picture and to the grown woman in the mirror. I still do."

Time spent in nature was a significant factor in helping Zoey to put herself back together. "I needed to not only think differently, I needed to be nourished in many ways. Beauty outside of me helped to restore the sense of beauty inside of me."

She also forgave her parents. "They didn't realize what they were doing," she said. "In fact, they thought they were doing their very best by teaching me to be strong, serious, and self-sufficient."

Similar to the way a kaleidoscope works, Zoey took what had seemed like broken parts, lifted them toward the light, looked from a new perspective, and, at long last, saw beauty within herself.

Then like a kaleidoscope, Zoey turned what she held into continuous patterns of beauty in her life.

How?

One day, at a teachers' conference about adolescence, Zoey learned that 60 percent of all girls experience a significant loss of self-esteem during their teen years. Many never gain it back. Zoey shuddered when she heard those statistics and thought about what can happen when a girl's sense of worth is diminished.

She knew from her own experience what low self-esteem felt like... what it was like to feel broken inside.

From her place of restored wholeness and her position as a teacher, Zoey created a program for girls making the transition from middle school to high school. She gives young girls many tools to help them build and maintain self-esteem in the face of threats to it. She encourages girls to support—rather than diminish—one another. She shows them ways to empower themselves.

Zoey's program has become an annual event in her community. Other schools have started similar programs modeled on her work. As a result, hundreds of girls, perhaps thousands now, have seen themselves in new ways—for the beauty that they are, and for the beauty that they possess. Many have experienced transformations. Many have said they feel more whole. Many of the girls' mothers have been positively affected by the program too.

Beauty

Zoey's example invites me to see how I too might take what seems like broken bits, raise them toward the light, look from a new perspective, and turn them into delightful patterns of beauty.

Beauty at Auschwitz

In 1943, at age 29, Etty Hillesum was sent with her family to the gas chambers at Auschwitz. Like Anne Frank, Etty kept a diary.

I like to hold in my mind an image of Etty as she describes herself "standing in some corner of the camp, my feet planted on earth, my eyes raised towards heaven, tears running down my face, tears of deep emotion and gratitude."

Gratitude!

In my mind's eye, I try to picture young Etty—malnourished, perhaps abused and bruised and yet appreciating the goodness and beauty of life. In my imagination, I stand by her side, and I wonder: What might she be appreciating in the moment? Is it something in nature? Does she see a purple wildflower pushing its way through parched soil? Has she spotted a deer in the distance? Has she heard the lilting call of a bird to its mate? Might the formation of clouds in the sky above offer a lovely sight to behold? Or, might a happy memory be uplifting her?

Any or all of those things, at times, may have stirred gratitude and joy in Etty's heart. However, I sense in her a capacity and a commitment to seeing beauty, and expressing beauty, no matter what. In fact, she also wrote, "I know what may lie in wait for us... And yet I find life beautiful and meaningful."

Etty's perspective leads me to think: *Surely, no matter what I face today, I too can find life beautiful.*

Touchstones

"Everything has its beauty, but not everyone sees it."
—CONFUCIUS

"Difficult times have helped me understand… how infinitely rich and beautiful life is in every way."
—ISAK DINESEN

"I do not think of all the misery, but of the glory that remains… Think of the beauty that again and again discharges itself within and without you and be happy."
—ANNE FRANK

For Reflection, Journaling, and Discussion

1. What are some ways that you experience beauty? Perhaps by listening to music? Arranging flowers? Volunteering?

2. In what places do you see beauty?

3. Do you sense your own beauty? Both inner and outer? Are you comfortable with both?

4. Recall a time when you acted with beauty. How did you feel?

5. Into what situations and areas of your life would you like to bring more beauty?

Courage

May you speak and act with confidence
and use courage to find your own path.

One Hero's Journey

Penny phoned from Oklahoma to share her story. For twenty years, while raising her children and managing her husband's office, she felt there was *something more* she was supposed to do with her life. Like many adult men and women, she joked, "I'm still trying to figure out what I want to be when I grow up."

One day Penny overheard someone ask her teenage daughter, "What does your mom do?"

"She runs," her daughter answered.

"She's a professional runner?" the acquaintance asked.

"Oh, no," her daughter laughed. "She runs stuff. She runs my dad's business. She runs our home. She runs me around. She runs everything."

That was a wake-up call for Penny, nudging her to find her *something more*.

Penny spent months researching, reflecting, and praying for guidance. Her search for direction included going on a pilgrimage to Jerusalem. There, she had an epiphany. For years, whenever Penny heard complaints about the weather, the economy, and the limited opportunities in her hometown of Muskogee, Oklahoma, she wished *someone* would help people appreciate the richness of their heartland community. In Jerusalem, Penny heard an inner voice say, *Why not you, Penny? Everywhere is holy land.* Penny decided to go home and do what she had wanted *someone* to do.

Even though she had no training or experience in television, Penny felt led to produce and host a morning show that would feature the talent, beauty, and strength—the gifts—of local residents. After writing a business plan, she met with a banker who gave her a litany of reasons why her inspirational, *Oprah*-like show would fail. He then stood to signal the end of the meeting and said, "I hope I have deterred you, Penny, because you won't last a week."

Choking back tears, Penny responded, "On the contrary. You have convinced me: *I absolutely need to do this!*"

So, Penny went ahead, funding the show herself, while she built advertising support to cover the expenses, which she kept to a minimum. She encountered many obstacles along the way and conceded that the banker was right… about some things. She was naïve; she made mistakes. But, she also learned.

"Most importantly, I learned how to tap into courage in order to be myself," she said.

According to Penny, her first taped shows were awful. "I was stiff and fake, trying to be like Oprah." But, when Penny did her first live show, she spoke from her heart and discovered the power of being herself.

One day, a jazz band was among her guests. Ten minutes before the show, in a moment alone,

Penny heard a song forming in her mind—*I've got the positive bluuuuues… I see the glass half fullll*—and she laughed. A moment later, an inner voice said, *Sing it on air, Penny.* She had not sung out loud in front of others since she was a child. In fact, Penny confessed that whenever she sang in church, she did it softly, so she wouldn't be heard by those around her.

Disregarding her past resistance to singing in public, Penny told the band about the song and asked if they would give her back up.

"We're with you, Penny. Go for it!" they urged.

The show started. Penny planned to introduce the song after the break. But during that break, she felt a twinge of fear. So did her husband. In fact, he was so afraid she would embarrass herself that he left the studio. His reaction led her to question herself.

I have a terrible singing voice. What am I thinking?

"In the past I would not have taken the risk," Penny said. "And I almost didn't. But suddenly I knew: *I have to ignore the fear!*"

In spite of her apprehensions, Penny did sing on air that day. She pushed through the fear. And when she did, she took another huge step on her hero's journey in reclaiming her voice... this time quite literally.

As we ended that telephone conversation, Penny summed up her perspective on courage in a way that touched upon nearly all The Twelve Gifts.

"Each of us is a magnificent creation," she said. "But we're all so afraid to let people see who we really are. How often do we discourage one another, instead of celebrating our efforts? How often do we turn away from watching an awkward child dance? How often do we avoid eye contact when a person speaks nervously? Who said we have to have pretty voices to sing? In heaven, all our voices sound beautiful!"

Penny's TV show aired for three years. Although the program never earned money for Penny, it provided enormous profit to her and to the community, as the richness of Muskogee was celebrated, just as Penny had wished *someone* would do.

Do It!

One Saturday afternoon, my husband, Frank, and I saw an advertisement for a "colossal RV sale" and decided to take a look, just for fun. After stepping in and out of a few models, we started to play like children, sitting in the driver and passenger seats and imagining scenic vistas and signs welcoming us to each of the lower 48 states.

After a while, we became quiet, explored models on our own, and looked at prices. On the way home, I said, "I have a crazy idea."

Reading my mind, Frank said, "Maybe it's not so crazy."

We mused over the possibilities of giving up our home, living in a motor home, and Frank taking a sabbatical from work. I could read and discuss the message of *The Twelve Gifts of Birth* with thousands of children, promote the book, and we could see the country.

The seemingly impossible dream became plausible when a company called to negotiate a large order and ended up purchasing a huge number of copies. Although they paid only a small amount per book, it could finance the trip and allow Frank to leave his work for a year and focus fully on what was fast becoming our mission.

Before buying a motor home, I called a best-selling author who had used an RV to promote his book. His advice to me was, "Don't do it! Imagine your house in an earthquake every day. That's what it's like when you're rumbling down highways."

I then called the president of a small press company who had also used a motor home to market a bestseller. He offered some encouragement but counseled me that even a small regional tour takes an immense amount of planning, coordination, and follow-up. He had a whole staff working on it. Did I have enough help?

Despite the cautions, with courage we went ahead and moved from 2,500 square feet of living space into 250.

On a sweltering summer Sunday in July 1999, we merged onto I-10 in Phoenix and began a one-year journey throughout America. Frank gripped the wheel with intense focus while I watched the white road lines. On both sides of our vehicle the lines seemed dangerously close, too easy to cross.

In setting out on this mission, had we crossed a line? I wondered.

After a while our tense muscles eased a bit. We even began to sing. Suddenly we heard a pop, felt a jarring shift, and smelled ruptured rubber. My stomach clenched. *A flat tire at 40 miles into a 40,000 mile trip? Are we making a big mistake? Maybe that author was right.*

In many ways both the author and the publisher were right. There were many challenges. The balancing jacks came down from the RV's undercarriage while we were driving. Low clearance bridges forced detours. On our way to Salt Lake City, on the day the first ever recorded tornado hit the city, high winds ripped away one of our awnings. Pipes froze during a cold night in West Virginia. There were many challenges with email, regular mail, and telephone communication. (Cellular technology was nascent compared to now. GPS was in its infancy.) We often had to climb up onto the roof for cell phone connection. Water leaked through the roof onto our computer during a heavy rainstorm and destroyed data. Forwarded snail mail got lost.

Creating a schedule was hard. Following it was harder. Days were long. TV interviews, when I could get them, were on early morning shows. In late morning and early afternoon we visited schools, shelters, and other community facilities.

Bookstore events started at 7 P.M. Many times we didn't get situated on a site, hooked up, and in bed until after 11. Then, all too often—because campgrounds are often near railroad tracks—the roar, whistle, and thundering vibration of a nearby passing train caused a sleep-interrupted night.

Fortunately, we were safe and could usually laugh at the adventure of it all. Always, the positives outweighed the negatives. Many other nights, when we were able to camp away from populated areas, we gazed at the star-studded sky and pondered our place in it all. We appreciated the diverse American landscape as we drove from place to place, crossing mountains, rivers, plains, and prairies.

One day near the end of the tour, as I was about to enter a bookstore, I noticed in the front window a copy of the book written by that author who had said, "Don't do it!" I stopped in my tracks and recalled my conversation with him. Glimpses of the past year played in my mind like clips from a movie. I saw ways that Frank and I had worked together to solve problems. I saw visits to national landmarks, like Mt. Rushmore in South Dakota, and sacred places, like the Weston Priory in Vermont. I saw faces of people we had met and new friends we had made. There were so many things we would never have experienced had we heeded that cautious advice.

I was so grateful that we had found the courage to say, *Do It!*

Through the Eyes of a Friend

J ack didn't recognize courage in himself until he was sixty years old. Up until then he thought that courage applied to heroes he learned about in history or saw featured on the nightly news. Other people. When a friend matter-of-factly commented on his courage, Jack was perplexed. He saw himself as an outgoing, creative guy, a family man with strong faith, but definitely not courageous. But when his lifelong friend explained how some of Jack's choices and actions looked through his eyes, Jack saw himself differently.

When Jack was a young man in his early twenties during the 1960s, he had tried to work in his father's insurance business, as was expected of him. His two older brothers fit in easily and seemed to enjoy their work. But Jack was bored with annuities, actuary tables, and other aspects of the industry. "It was worse than being bored," he said. "I felt like I was dying inside."

Jack felt drawn to hair styling and dreamed of owning a salon with a lively environment. He was sure that he would enjoy the creative and social aspects of it and that he'd be successful. When he was twenty-six, Jack approached his father and expressed his intentions of leaving the business and going to cosmetology school. As Jack anticipated, his father raged and accused Jack of being selfish, ungrateful, and unmanly. Despite the fiery temper, Jack loved his father. In the face of his father's fury, Jack felt confusion and fear. His resolve wavered. But then a force filled his chest and he stood firm in his decision.

In following his path, Jack not only built three flourishing salons, but in the midst of the outer beauty business, Jack often helped clients experience their inner beauty by listening and encouraging them when they faced dark times. His love for his work led to donating time and talent at nursing homes, which in turn led to becoming a hospice volunteer, and eventually to steering fundraising efforts for the hospice program in his community.

With a shifted perspective as a result of looking in the "mirror" offered by his friend, Jack saw that he had used courage in choosing his own career and in other situations.

When, after having two healthy children of their own, Jack and his wife, Michele, decided to bring an orphaned Korean child into their family, his father threatened to disown them. Jack understood that for reasons he could not comprehend, his father feared adoption, in this case especially because the child was of a different racial background than their family. Jack and Michele risked rejection and went ahead with the adoption. It took years but eventually the patriarch loved the little girl and accepted his son's independent choices.

Through his friend's view, Jack realized that, although he often felt fear and still does, he has always had courage. In fact, courage was the scaffolding around which he had built richness into his life.

Choosing Life

Olivia is one of dozens of women who have shared stories of using courage to first cope with, then escape from, and eventually heal and grow from abusive and toxic relationships. Olivia compared her situation to a frog that is placed in a pot of cold water on a stove. Little by little, the water heats, and the frog adjusts to the increase of temperature without jumping out of the pot. Had that frog been immersed initially in water near the boiling point, he would have instinctively hopped out.

"I didn't see that side of him when we were courting or first married," said Olivia. "The harshness, the criticism, the belittling, the sarcasm, the meanness, the controlling… it all started slowly. And then it grew and grew and reached a level that was like boiling water for the frog."

In sharing her story, Olivia avoided referring to her ex-husband by name and refrained from describing specific incidents.

"That time of my life is over," she said. "I don't want to revisit the details and dwell in the past or judge my former husband. I want to now focus only on the good. I'm so grateful that I realized that, like that little frog in the pot, my spirit was dying in that relationship."

For years Olivia considered leaving the toxic situation; but the vows she had taken kept her trying to improve the marriage. Even after accepting the reality that her husband was not honoring those vows, she had no idea how she would survive on her own. And so she hesitated.

Olivia said that once she arrived at the decision to leave that marriage, she felt a big inner shift. "Or maybe it was the other way around," she said. "Maybe I felt the shift in my heart and then the decision in my head happened. Either way, there was no more waffling. I still didn't know *how* things were going to work out. But there was a moment when I absolutely chose to live. In that moment, I was filled with courage and with confidence that the way would be shown to me. And it was."

Olivia's story and those of dozens of other women who escaped harsh situations, some despite enormous social pressure, some under cover of night, some with children in tow, demonstrate something. Whether it is to leave a toxic place, or to live authentically, or to publish a book, or to climb a mountain, in the moment of commitment, we are met by Spirit, filled with courage, and often assisted in ways we never imagined.

"It takes courage to grow up and turn
out to be who you truly are."

—E.E. CUMMINGS

"You gain strength, courage, and confidence by
every experience in which you really look fear in
the face… You must do the thing you cannot do."

—ELEANOR ROOSEVELT

"Many of our fears are tissue-paper thin, and a single
courageous step would carry us clear through them."

—BRENDAN FRANCIS

"Back where I come from, we have men
who are called heroes… and they have
no more courage than you have."

—WIZARD OF OZ

For Reflection, Journaling, and Discussion

1. Recall a time when you used courage to "follow your own path."

2. Consider your most heartfelt dreams. Is there something you feel called to do *that you have not yet acted upon... because you feel afraid?*

3. How might you nurture your dreams with courage?

4. Into what situations and areas of your life would you like to bring more courage?

Compassion

May you be gentle with yourself and others.
May you forgive those who hurt you
and yourself when you make mistakes.

The Kindness One

"The kindness one." I remember the first time I heard that phrase.

I had just begun to visit schools and shelters in my home state of Arizona, reading and discussing my first book, *The Twelve Gifts of Birth*, with children. Sitting in a kindergarten-sized, wooden chair at a children's home in Tucson, I faced ten attentive little boys sitting on the floor in a semi-circle in front of me.

Completing the story, I asked, "What gift seems most important to you? Do you have a favorite one?"

"The kindness one!" chimed the youngest boy. "The kindness one!" he said again with enthusiasm, raising his chin from its resting place on his fists and stretching tall from his crossed-ankles position. He didn't yet know the word "compassion," but he knew what it meant and he recognized it as the most important gift, from his four-year-old perspective. Yes, he was only four; yet he registered a strong sense of what compassion looks like and feels like, when he recognized gentleness and caring between brothers in one of the book's photos.

A few months later, I heard it again: *the kindness one*.

It was in a third-grade class starting a new school year, just four months after the Columbine shootings, in Denver, Colorado, not far from Littleton. After listening to my story and hearing the question, "What gift seems most important to you?" without hesitation a seven-year-old boy answered, "The kindness one."

Throughout my tour through America, whenever I visited schools, many young children chose compassion—either by naming "compassion" or calling it "the kindness one"—as the gift they thought was most important.

When I recall those children, I experience appreciation and awe for their innate wisdom, especially at their tender, young ages. I have often wondered how many acts of violence could have been prevented if only "the kindness one" had been valued and cultivated in those who committed the acts; if only they had experienced more kindness in their own lives; if only they were helped to understand that we all, at times, experience deep emotional pain.

What might this world be like if "the kindness one" had been valued and nurtured in all of us? What might our lives be like if, starting now, we each practice kindness every day toward ourselves and others?

Margaret's Ah-ha Moment

Margaret from Pennsylvania told me about an experience she'd had thirty years ago, when she was in her early twenties. One day, during a time of depression and uncertainty, she'd suddenly realized that everyone who is now living, as well as everyone who has ever lived, had a sense of how she felt because they, too, have felt emotional pain and confusion at some point in their lives.

"In that moment, I became aware that thousands, millions, maybe a billion, maybe *billions* of people on the planet were hurting in some way right then, at the same time as I was," she said. "Even though they did not know me personally, they knew how I felt and I knew how they felt... not exactly, but we all knew pain. In that moment, my heart burst open. I felt compassion for them and compassion for me. I try to remember that experience whenever I sink into depression and feel alone in my own sadness. It helps me to be kinder to myself and to others."

Forgiveness

Kathy from Illinois shared a story that serves as a reminder to watch for little hostilities and negative judgments that pop up every day and to turn them into opportunities to grow in compassion.

"For years I hated myself," she said. "Early in my childhood, I got the impression that I was unloved and unlovable. There were so many situations during my growing up years that stirred feelings of shame in me. My dad drank, my mom had an affair with a neighbor, my parents divorced, and my mom married the neighbor, to name a few. Like many children living in unhappy homes, I misunderstood what was happening and felt that I was somehow to blame."

Little by little, through reading, counseling, retreats, and educational programs, Kathy learned to let go of the negative judgments she had of herself—and of her parents—and to allow healing to happen.

"I finally *got it*," she said. "Not just the intellectual concept that none of it was my 'fault.' I really saw, felt, and understood how I had been holding false and limiting beliefs about myself. And I let them go. Then I started to feel genuine love, tenderness, and kindness toward Little Kathy, Teenage Kathy, Young Adult Kathy, me in all my stages, and me *now*. I'm still letting go of false beliefs. Whenever I catch myself falling into an old pattern of self-criticism, hostility, or negative judgment, I stop, forgive myself, and deliberately speak kindly to Little Kathy—who still hurts sometimes—and to me now."

Kathy says she has also fully forgiven her parents.

"Actually, I have forgiven *myself* for judging them as bad parents, and, as a result, freedom, peace, and joy have come to me. The truth is: my parents were doing the best they could at the time. They were hurting too. My intention now is to accept myself and everyone else, just as we are."

Apples and Oranges

Way back when my daughters were in elementary school, more than twenty-five years ago, I noticed a difference in the way one of my husband's uncles and one of my uncles treated the children in our families. My uncle, Ray, paid close attention to what even very young children said. He genuinely enjoyed playing checkers, engaging in paddle ball contests, and watching our children as they proudly performed a newly learned skill, such as twirling a baton. My husband's uncle, Spike, didn't relate as well to children. In fact, sometimes he was dismissive and gruff toward them. And so I judged him as "unkind" and "not good enough" with children.

One summer day, we had a serious plumbing problem in our home. The basement in our century-old Victorian farmhouse was filled with sewage back-up. As soon as he heard about it, Uncle Spike showed up in hip boots, prepared to help drain and clean the basement. He showed no reluctance or reservation about dealing with the mess and the stench.

Again, I compared the uncles. What I saw led me closer to accepting and appreciating people as they are. While my Uncle Ray was great with kids, he could not fix a thing, and he certainly would not have been willing to enter that basement and try. The sight of Uncle Spike in his hip boots clearly illustrated for me that we all have different skills and personalities. We all have different strengths and weaknesses. We all have our particular ways of showing love. We're all here to learn.

Compassion

"If we could read the secret history of our enemies,
we should find in each man's life, sorrow and
suffering enough to disarm all hostility."
—HENRY WADSWORTH LONGFELLOW

A man is seeking money
He is living on the street
I see his sign and judge
Thinking he'll drink instead of eat
I start to turn the corner when I turn to see his face
I see the God within him, I place 20 on his plate

Throughout the day they come
Moments meant for me
Throughout the day life lays them at my feet
She says, "Have compassion"
She says, "Take the risk"
She says, "Go on and love the one you're with"

A spider in the bathtub
A fly upon the wall
A traffic jam, the couple, fighting

Touchstones

Somewhere down the hall
The man who cut before me
The waitress late and rude
Within these golden moments
Lies a fundamental truth

To get the love I want
I must give the love I seek
As I do for you, my friend
Someone will do for me
These laws of love are written
They're embedded in the heart
So what stands right here before me
Is the perfect place to start...

For Reflection, Journaling, and Discussion

1. Recall a time when your heart opened and you felt compassion for yourself. Recall a time when you felt compassion for someone else.

2. Did you act upon these instances in some way? How do you feel, now, as you're remembering it?

3. In what ways do you presently show kindness to yourself?

4. What judgments about yourself and others, if any, are you ready to release?

5. Into what situations and areas of your life would you like to bring more compassion?

Hope

*Through each passage and season, may
you trust the goodness of life.*

Despite Appearances

One day, many years ago, my husband, young daughters, and I noticed an unusual silence in the house when we returned home from a family party. Usually our zebra finch, named Cubby, greeted us with song whenever the front door of our house opened or closed.

Cubby was a sweet and colorful little bird—with black, white, and grey stripes and a spot of bright orange that seemed to represent his outgoing personality. We could always count on him to respond to the squeaks of the door's hinges with squeaks of his own.

That night, however, he made no sound. We found him lying on the bottom of his cage, completely still.

Cubby had lived well beyond the average life span of zebra finches and long after his mate had died. We were thankful for that. And we planned to bury him the next day.

In the morning, although Cubby was still motionless on the bottom of the cage, he was upright, not lying on his side like the night before. With his head tucked down and his body pulled in toward its center, he took the form of a downy, feathered ball. Although he seemed barely alive, surprisingly, he was alive!

If this happened today, I would probably take the little bird to the vet for help. But back then, I thought that vets were only for dogs, cats, horses, and farm animals. And so we let nature takes its course.

For days, Cubby stayed in that downy-ball position on the bottom of the cage. Then, slowly, he began to move about. With awe, we watched him recuperate. For a long time, Cubby lived quietly, in a limited way, on the bottom of his cage. Finally, he hopped up to a higher perch and seemed back to his old self, in all ways but one: he no longer sang.

Months passed.

One bright Sunday morning, the front door was opened, and Cubby again echoed the squeak! For two more years, the little zebra finch filled our home with song.

That experience, in and of itself, is a touchstone for me. And there is more to this story.

A year after Cubby died, my mother had a severe stroke. My husband, our daughters, and I flew to be with her. We were told she had very little time.

Upon arriving at the hospital, I hardly recognized my mom. When I asked about her prognosis, her doctor shook his head and lowered his eyes, avoiding mine.

"What are you telling me, doctor?" I asked.

"It was massive," he said. "You should prepare yourself."

Sometime during that restless night, as I cried and prayed for her peaceful passing, a voice within jolted me. *Remember Cubby,* it said. *Where there is life, there is hope.*

I remembered how the life force within that little bird had directed his healing. I began to pray for life to remain with my mother and for its force to heal her. I also prayed for peace when life would leave her body, whenever that time would come.

Despite her appearance and the dismal predictions of her doctor and the intensive care staff, my mother—like Cubby—pulled through; and as time passed, her healing progressed. In less than two years, my mother fully recovered. In many ways she was more healthy and active than she had been before the stroke. Every day she walked three miles through a park near her home, enjoying the beauty of nature. She lived to see the graduations of her granddaughters from high school and college, the birth of a grandson, and so much more, while she continued to enrich our lives.

Yes, where there is life, there is hope.

Going with the Flow in Fargo

Late in the day on September 3, 1999, my husband and I arrived, in our motor home, at Lindenwood Park in Fargo, North Dakota. We were ready to set up camp, go to bed early, and get a good night's sleep.

"This rain is predicted to continue all night," said the campground official at the gate. "But don't worry. If the river gets too high, we'll come to your site and advise you to evacuate."

I slept very little that night—not only because we were parked right next to the rising Red River; I was also kept awake by the trees that towered above us. Sometime during the night, the heavy downpour began to carry, along with rain, a steady flow of acorns. Each one that hit the roof did so with a loud *Ping!* It seemed as if those tall oaks released

a million acorns that night. *Ping!—Ping!—Ping!...*
Ping!—Ping!—Ping!... Ping!—Ping!—Ping! At one
point I wondered, *How can there be any more acorns
left to fall?*

In the early morning, nearing the time I was
supposed to call a local radio station for a scheduled
five-minute interview, the cacophony of rain and
acorns continued. Sleep deprived, I panicked.

"How will I hear the interviewer? Will this
racket be heard by listeners?" I asked my husband.
"Will we even have a cell connection in this weather?"

I checked the phone. It turned out that we did
not have a connection. So, I couldn't even call the
station to explain the problem.

"Don't worry," Frank said. "It will work out.
Get up and get dressed. We'll drive there."

"Drive where? We don't know where it is. I don't
have time to shower," I continued with my concerns.

After quickly dressing himself and urging me to
do the same, he went out into the storm to unhook
the electric and water connections. I worried about
that too—Frank handling the electric line while

standing in the pouring rain. *This is not good,* I kept thinking. *Not good.*

When Frank was safely back inside, suddenly something shifted in me. There was no more fear, anxiety, or resistance to the situation. It was what it was. And like the rain and acorns, I was willing to be in the flow. Whatever happened was fine… better than fine. It would be good. It already was good.

I don't remember how, but we found the station with ease. But, the main door was locked, and no staff person was in sight. After knocking repeatedly on that door, Frank circled around the building and tried other doors. Finally, at one door, someone heard and let us in.

I was wet, poorly groomed, and without an invitation for an in-studio interview. Nevertheless, I was warmly welcomed by the team on-air, handed a headset, and drawn in to their lively banter.

Not only did I relax and have fun, I got to be a part of the entire show instead of just a five-minute piece of it. The bookstore event that afternoon was packed with people who had heard the show.

Although we "lived" in Fargo for only one day, on that day I felt as if I was truly a part of the community. And although our challenge alongside the rising Red River was a mild one, I felt connected to all the people who face flooding there, and everywhere.

The memory of that day encourages me to trust that we are, indeed, all connected, and to go with the flow, as best I can, with hope.

Falling into Place

In 1994, my mom was diagnosed with leukemia. For the next three years she worked toward wellness. Despite a grim prognosis, she believed it was possible to release the malignant leukemia cells from her body. She hoped for a cure.

One morning, Mom recognized that she was not going to "get better." Simply and silently, she shared with me her sense of going downhill. With tear-filled eyes, she shook her head back and forth and gestured thumbs down. Silence filled the room like a third presence with us. We both just let that silence be, while I held my mom and she held me.

"What do I do now?" she finally said. "There is nothing more for me to do."

I didn't know how to answer. It was true; there was little she could *do*. She had already ceased activities that had shaped her daily life, activities in which she had found great pleasure, such as cooking and cleaning—my mom had loved housework. Now, there was also no more "fighting" the leukemia.

My mom didn't seem to expect an answer, but from a place within herself she heard one: *Anna, you don't have to do anything. Just be.*

"Oh," she said to that, and thought about it for awhile.

Later, another question emerged in her, one that was not rhetorical. It was a real question, posed to God. "What would you have me learn today?" she asked every morning for the rest of her life. And she got answers.

During those last weeks, my mom often said, "Oh," and, "Oh, I see."

What did she see? I didn't know. Although my mom didn't share what she saw, she conveyed a lot with a few simple words, facial expressions, and gestures.

When she said, "Oh," and, "I see," her eyes brightened like a child grasping the meaning of fractions, or learning to read, or balancing on a bike for the first time. Several times, with a knowing smile, while her hands moved as if she were putting together an invisible puzzle, she said, "Everything is falling into place, Charlene."

Perhaps she was seeing scenes from her life within a new context, one that showed her the meaning behind previous confusions and hurts.

I never learned what my mom saw, but I saw her peace-filled response to it. Despite the frailty of her ravaged body, beauty and joy shone through my mom as she saw "answers." And the memory of that always deepens my sense of hope. It stirs within me the certainty that, on some level, the pieces are *always* in place. It encourages me, no matter what is happening, to trust in what is unfolding and to trust in the goodness of life.

"Hope is not the conviction that something will turn out well, but the certainty that something makes sense, regardless of how it turns out."
—VACLAV HAVEL

"Hope is seated in our hearts to help us live with the tension between our wishes and desires on one hand and our disappointments, tragedies, and despair on the other."
—CAREN GOLDMAN

"No pessimist ever discovered the secrets of the stars, or sailed to an uncharted land, or opened a new heaven to the human spirit."
—HELEN KELLER

"All shall be well, and all shall be well, and all manner of things shall be well."
—JULIAN OF NORWICH

"Find the good and praise it."
—ALEX HAILEY

For Reflection, Journaling, and Discussion

1. Recall a time when your hopes for a certain outcome were met.

2. Recall a time when circumstances did not turned out as you wished, but with hindsight, you recognized the outcome as "good."

3. Consider asking, each morning upon your awakening: *What would you have me learn today?*

4. Into what situations and areas of your life would you like to bring more hope?

Joy

May it keep your heart open and filled with light.

White Sand and Yellow Stones

Driving on our way "down the shore" (the Jersey shore), we would cross a bridge that spanned high above a wide river. Even as a small child, sitting low in the backseat, barely able to peer out the window, not yet knowing the name of the bridge, or the river, or the cities on both sides, I noticed changes, both within and outside of me, as a result of crossing that bridge.

As soon as our car rolled on to the bridge, I felt a sense of leaving behind "city stuff." At the peak of the span, I would look back and say a grateful good-bye to the puffing smokestacks that lined the river's far side. Then I would eagerly look ahead for my first glimpse of sand on the "other side."

Although the trip would take a while longer, it seemed as if "the shore" started right there, on that "other side" of the bridge, where great mounds of sand stood. Even though my first glimpse was of sand at an industrial site, not yet at the beach, those mounds of white sand held promise and never failed to stir joy in me.

From there, it got better and better, as we ventured deeper into "the shore" region, where white sand appeared naturally in the soil lining the roads and yellow stones encircled the houses.

Every day, rain or shine, those yellow stones seemed to cast sunlight up from the ground. On cloudy days, I would look to them and feel the sunshine near my feet. And I would watch the stones for changes. I could better detect the return of sunshine by looking to the stones than by looking to the sky. In their subtle lightening and brightening, the stones were the first objects in the environment to foretell the clearings of clouds.

I know now that the bridge is the Driscoll, the river is the Raritan, and the cities north and south of the river are Perth Amboy and South Amboy. I don't yet know the proper geological name for what

Joy

are commonly called "yellow shore stones." Most importantly, I *do* know that turning my attention to what reflects even just a hint of light in the world will stir an uplift of joy in my soul.

Is That You, Mommy?

"I was feeling sorry for myself," Nancy said, as she began to tell me about her touchstone for joy. "I was missing the excitement of my job. It seemed as if life was passing me by."

For ten years, Nancy had been building a career in radio. In fact, she had worked her way up to producing one of the top radio shows in Los Angeles. Then, Nancy's daughter was born, and her time away from work stretched from a five-month maternity leave to a five-year sabbatical.

"It was my choice," Nancy said. "I wanted to give my full attention to my daughter until she started school. Nevertheless, on that particular day, I was missing the world 'out there.' Pushing the stroller around my neighborhood—*again*—was boring. I longed for adult camaraderie. I wanted to experience the challenges of production and the adrenaline of radio."

Nancy's mind often wandered during those walks though her neighborhood. On that particular day, feeling sorry for herself, Nancy fantasized about getting a nanny and returning to work sooner.

The sweet little voice of her two-year-old child interrupted Nancy's musings.

"Is that you there, Mommy?"

"Yes, honey."

"I happy Mommy."

According to Nancy, in that moment she felt as if she had been raised above the ground and spun around in a complete circle. When she seemed to have come back down and her feet touched earth again, Nancy sensed herself to be in a whole new place, with a changed perspective. She was fully present.

"I'm happy too, sweetheart!" said Nancy. And she meant it, fully.

The Master Key

During my cancer-healing journey, I discovered that I could experience joy each day, no matter what was happening. Even in the midst of depression, frustration, anger, confusion, or chemotherapy side-effects, I was able to get in touch with joy because I had found a key for opening myself to joy. Little rainbows led me to it.

Across the room from my bed, a cut-crystal bowl sat on a table, under a window that faced southeast. At a certain time, nearly every morning (every morning that the sun shone, which was nearly every day in Phoenix), sunlight passed through the bowl. As it did, the light was refracted. For a few moments, that refracted light caused hundreds of tiny arched rainbows to appear on my walls. Always, when I saw them, I experienced joy.

Joy

One cloudy day, when the rainbows did not appear, I thought of them and how much I appreciated them. Even though they were not present on my walls in that moment, gratitude for them *was* present in that moment. And, in that moment, I noticed a sense of opening in my heart, followed by an uplift of joy.

From there I began to notice that whenever I felt genuine gratitude for anything, I automatically felt joy. I also learned that I could not force gratitude to be present. Pretend gratitude did not work.

So I learned to sit, be present, look around, watch, and wait. Sure enough, eventually, always, I would notice something for which I was truly grateful. It might be for the mesquite tree outside my window, for the birds that flew to and from it, for the celery-green color of the bedroom walls, for the pillows supporting my back. No matter how seemingly small the object or situation, when I felt grateful for it, I experienced the opening to joy.

Now, every night, before turning off the light, I look around my room, and look back upon my day,

with the intention of noticing anything and everything for which I am genuinely grateful, right in the
moment. Some nights it's a lot; some nights it's not.
But there is always something. And coming upon it
with complete authenticity is a bit like seeing those
little rainbows suddenly appearing on my walls.

I recently heard gratitude referred to as "the
master key." I know that it can be a key for opening
joy. It might very well be a key for opening all of
life's gifts.

Bucket List

I met Kay at The Wellness Community in Phoenix. Like me, Kay had been diagnosed with cancer. For Kay, it was pancreatic cancer.

Most people who hear "pancreatic cancer" may conclude that death is near, within a year. Kay did too, at first. So, she asked herself, "What do I want to do before I die?" She reviewed the things that had been on her "Life-To-Do List" and started acting upon them.

For example, even though Kay lived in "The Grand Canyon State," she had not yet hiked in the Grand Canyon. She had not even *visited* the Grand Canyon. Determined to live the best life she could until she died, Kay and her husband made the trip north and, with great care and joy, hiked together down onto the floor of the canyon from the North

Rim, stayed overnight, and hiked up on the South Rim side the next day. "My husband practically had to carry me out. But we did it!" Kay told me.

That was the first of many activities Kay got to cross off her "Bucket List," including riding in a hot air balloon over the Phoenix Valley and learning sign language. But there was no way she was going to be able to cross off working in the Peace Corps. Or was there?

At first, Kay thought she would have to abandon that dream completely. Certainly, she would not be able to actually *join* the Peace Corps. However, when Kay learned of a short-term mission project that her church was planning, she said, "I could do *that!*" And she did. By joining a group of volunteers and helping to repair a church, a school, a hospital, and several houses in Puerto Rico, Kay fulfilled the *essence* of her Peace Corps dream.

"I felt extremely grateful and joyful to have that opportunity," Kay said. "And for finding ways to experience everything on my list, including teaching children at a cancer camp for kids and becoming a patient advocate."

Kay largely credits joy for her surviving well beyond the life span she and others expected after her diagnosis in 1994.

"Yup, 1994." Kay smiled. "Somehow, with the help of joy, gratitude, good medicine, and grace, I'm still here," she told me in 2004. "And, I'm still adding things to my list. And, I do simple things that stir the joy in me daily, like riding on the swing that my husband hung for me."

One March morning, a few years later, I visited with Kay again, via phone. She told me she and her husband had just taken down their Christmas tree.

"We love the little white lights. So, we left the tree up so we could enjoy watching them twinkle every night," she said. "In fact, instead of packing the lights away with the tree, I draped them around a large plant and hung eggs from it. We now have a twinkling 'Easter tree' to enjoy for a few months. After that, who knows where I'll put those lights?"

Her childlike delight was infectious, and my heart was uplifted by the end of our call.

"No matter what is happening, we can find ways to stir the joy in us," Kay says. "I've learned that joy gives me more strength, and more hope." She recommends making a list and doing at least one joy-stirring thing every day. "For example," she laughs and repeats, "I ride on that swing my husband hung for me!"

As of this writing, Kay is a seventeen-year pancreatic-cancer-survivor, still finding ways to live in joy every day. When I spoke with her this morning, she told me about the joy she experiences with her fifteen-month-old grandson, Dominic. "One of our favorite things to do together is to hold hands, run in the sunlight, and giggle. Simple, huh? And pure joy!"

Joy

"It is our basic right to be a happy person, happy family, and eventually a happy world. That should be our goal."

—DALAI LAMA

"We are born to delight in the world."

—CARL SAGAN

"Learning compassion, understanding love, and experiencing joy... That's our purpose. Our reason for being here. That's our true mission on the planet."

—MELODY BEATTIE

"Even during sad times, joy is within you. Bring it forth. Wisdom is there to guide you."

—FROM *THE TWELVE GIFTS FOR HEALING*

For Reflection, Journaling, and Discussion

Consider this quote:

> You can feel happy simply because you experience happiness in your nature... You can learn to be happy and not in conflict with others or situations, regardless of what is going on...If your happiness is misunderstood or judged by others, you can turn it to peace, understanding, and compassion by choosing to be happy, regardless.

—JOHN MORTON
FROM *YOU ARE THE BLESSINGS*

1. With what parts of it do you agree or disagree?

2. If you were to make a "Joy-Stirring List" what would be on it? (For example: dance, take a bath, walk barefoot, call a friend, play with a child or pet, etc.)

3. Into what situations and areas of your life would you like to bring more joy?

Talent

*May you discover your own special abilities
and contribute them toward a better world.*

Talentry

During the year I toured the United States, I asked thousands of school children to tell me about their gift of talent. In every classroom, hands shot up, and boys and girls exclaimed examples of art, athletics, and academics.

"I can draw!"

"I can sing!"

"I'm good at baseball!"

"I'm good at swimming!"

"I'm good at math!"

"I'm good at spelling!"

In all the places I visited, only one child said, "I don't have talent." In fact, that little girl yelled, *"I do not have talent!"*

"Why do you say that?" I asked.

She answered, "My mom says I'm good for nothing and she knows. My mom is smart."

For a moment I felt stunned. I didn't know what to say. It was so disheartening to hear this from a child. And yet I could relate. I hadn't heard I was "good for nothing"; however, I had sometimes felt "not good enough." Haven't we all?

I very much wanted to encourage the children—especially this little girl—to see themselves as valuable, inventive, creative—good at something, many things, in fact. But how? I felt guided to respect her response, proceed, and trust in what would unfold.

I asked the group, "What do you love to do? What makes you happy?"

With her arms wrapped tight across her chest, that little girl sat still as she watched the other children and heard their answers bursting forth like popcorn.

"I'm good at taking care of my baby brother!"

"I can make people laugh!"

"I'm good at putting puzzles together!"

"I like to look at the stars!"

"I know sign language!"

"I love my dog!"

"I can twirl my tongue!"

"Look, I can put my legs behind my head!"

Finally, she too contributed an answer.

"I like to brush my cat," she said.

Eventually all the children, including that little girl, named several things.

For me, these answers demonstrate that talent is more than skill in art, athletics, and academics. They also strengthen my conviction that we need to expand our understanding of talent, not minimize or deny it.

How many times have you heard someone say, "I don't have talent"? Have you ever said it yourself? Why, even Albert Einstein said, "I have no particular talent. I'm merely inquisitive."

But, it doesn't serve us—or the world—to be small, as Marianne Williamson so eloquently said. "We ask ourselves, 'Who am I to be brilliant, gorgeous, talented and fabulous?' Actually, who are you not to be? We are all meant… to manifest the glory of God that is within us."

I think we need a fresh, new way of looking at talent. Perhaps a new word would help. What if we use the expression "talentry" as we look for this gift in ourselves and others? "Talentry" can mean the broad, unique mix of abilities, interests, and potentials that exists in every human's makeup.

The challenges we face today are even greater than they were during 1999–2000, when I discussed talent with all those students who are now adults. It is critical that they—and we—all see ourselves as talented, inventive, creative, and able.

Remember Scarecrow in *The Wizard of Oz*? He thought he wasn't "smart." Although he wasn't brainy—he didn't even have a brain—he was a caring, natural leader and solved many of his little group's problems along their journey on the yellow brick road. Each of us can make the world a better place, especially when we use our true talentry.

It's Not Too Late to Excavate

After an overnight stay in a camping area at Homolovi State Park in Winslow, Arizona, I met several people toiling away at the archaeological dig site there. Among them was Betsy, a volunteer on the job. A beautiful older woman who resembled Katharine Hepburn, Betsy wore gauzy, light-colored clothing that fully covered her arms and legs. A wide-brimmed straw hat shaded her face and neck and provided further protection from the scorching summer sun. Despite the fierce heat, her advanced age, and plastic tubes in her nostrils to deliver oxygen from the cylinder at her side, Betsy exuded joy as she worked. With a small brush in hand, the tool for her delicate work, she gently and lovingly dusted layers of sand and soil from a long-buried wall. She explained that she had longed to do archeological work since she was twelve years old. In addition to strong interest and a sense of calling, young Betsy felt that she had the natural ability to patiently excavate the remains of ancient cultures.

However, as was common in those times, upon reaching young adulthood, she married and dedicated more than fifty years to raising children and helping with grandchildren. "I loved the family-raising part of my life," Betsy said. "Please don't misunderstand that. But now, I'm living my childhood dream!"

As I walked away, it occurred to me that Betsy's literal unearthing of a buried archaeological treasure symbolized an uncovering of her own talent. When I think of Betsy now, I wonder about the many aspects of talent that lie hidden within each one of us. Betsy's example also reminds me that it is never too late to excavate and discover treasures within our own trove of talent.

Little Things Matter

When the growth of leukemia cells in my mom's body began to increase rapidly, she was admitted to the hospital to receive a blood transfusion and be treated for an infection. After the procedures, she and I decided to take a little walk in the halls.

Slowly... *very* slowly... with one hand and arm resting on mine, the other hand pushing her IV pole, she made her way around the corridor, glancing into each room we passed. When a patient made eye contact, my mom smiled and said, "Hello." At the doorway of each sleeping patient, she paused, let go of the IV pole, and offered a little sign-of-the-cross blessing with her hand.

At the nurses' station, Mom stopped and thanked everyone for their care. Upon returning to her room,

I helped my mom back into bed. As her head touched the pillow, she was asleep.

For several minutes, I stood there, gazing at my mom's peaceful face. I reflected on how my mom, even in her weakened condition, was expressing a talent, *her* talent for caring about people. In those seemingly small and simple gestures, my mom was making a difference. She was bringing a measure of love and compassion into the world.

Someday Arrives

Sinking into the lounger next to my mom's hospital bed while she napped, I noticed the soft rays of September sunlight cascading across her body. Through the opened window, I heard the laughter of school children and the drone of a distant lawn mower. I breathed in the fragrance of fresh cut grass. Somehow, despite my mother's facing death, everything seemed right and beautiful in the world.

Instead of opening the book in my lap and reading to pass the time, I simply sat and observed. I considered the contrast between this unhurried experience and my usual harried lifestyle. I valued the kindness my mother had just demonstrated during our walk around the corridor.

All of a sudden, in the midst of the peace, I heard in my body: *What you do with your time and talent is critically important. Pay attention.* And I knew immediately what that meant.

After receiving numerous rejections for *The Twelve Gifts of Birth,* I had decided to give up—not on publishing altogether, just on selling the manuscript to an established publisher. I had resolved to do it myself… *someday.* For the past ten years *someday* had been a vague, elusive time in the future.

Now, I knew: *Someday* had arrived.

I realized that it would be a disservice to the book—which I felt had come *through* me and had not just been written *by* me—if I left it in a folder on my computer any longer. Since it was my intention to be of service with this work, I understood that I needed to honor that intention—and my time and talent—by following through, in whatever way was necessary.

I believe that the inner guidance I heard is true for you too. *What you do with your time and talent is critically important.* Might your *someday* be now?

Talent

*"Hide not your talents, they for use were made.
What's a sun-dial in the shade?"*

—Benjamin Franklin

*"Do not wish to be anything but what you
are, and try to be that perfectly."*

—St. Francis de Sales

"Follow your bliss."

—Joseph Campbell

For Reflection, Journaling, and Discussion

1. How do you presently perceive and define "talent"?

2. Do you consider yourself to "have talent"?

3. What everyday activities come easily to you? What brings you joy?

4. What did you love to do when you were a child? (For example: ride a bicycle, draw pictures, make music, read, play ball, make people laugh, build stuff, take stuff apart, play in the dirt, look at the stars, dance, etc.)

5. Is there a dream in your heart to which you have been saying, *Someday?*

6. Into what areas of your life would you like to bring more of your special abilities?

Imagination

May it nourish your visions and dreams.

The Diamondbacks

It was November 4, 2001. I was at home in Phoenix, sitting on the couch with my two cats curled next to me, while I watched the seventh game of the World Series between the Arizona Diamondbacks and the New York Yankees.

My husband and one of our daughters were downtown at the ballpark, among the 49,589 attendees. I didn't have the energy to join them. I *did* have enough energy, however, to jump up and down throughout the game and to yell and cheer when the Diamondbacks scored. Although I had been a Yankee fan in the past, my allegiance that night was with the hometown underdogs.

Following the burst of jubilation on the field after winning the World Series, a sportscaster interviewed then Arizona Diamondbacks' manager, Bob Brenly. In a tone suggesting his answer would be *no*, she said, "Did you ever *imagine* this during spring training?"

Bob hesitated for a moment, smiled graciously, and said, "Well, actually, yes. Yes, we did."

"Silly question," I said out loud at the interviewer—I had already been talking to the TV for the past few hours. "Doesn't every team *imagine winning* at the start of the season?!"

Yet, I understood her question. The Arizona win seemed unlikely. In existence only three years, this baseball team didn't have a history of success or much of a history at all. The odds were in favor of the legendary Yankees who had won twenty-seven World Series championships *and* had been in existence just about as long as Arizona had been a state!

Months passed. I found myself often reflecting on that post-game interview, the sportscaster's question, and the manager's answer. With a strong desire to know more about *how* the team imagined, I decided to try for my own interview.

So, I looked up the number, phoned the Arizona Diamondbacks, and asked to speak with Mr. Brenly.

Imagination

Apparently, my timing was perfect. He took my call, and for ten minutes or so, we had a lively conversation devoted to one idea: imagination.

"Imagination alone won't create success," the manager said. "In baseball, there are many other factors—skill, practice, determination. But, without it, there is *no* chance."

Mr. Brenly explained that at the start of the season, he had evaluated his team. Taking into account all the variables, he felt that they absolutely had a chance of winning—despite their newness. "In fact," he said, "I felt that, barring injuries, there was no reason why we *couldn't* win, as long as all twenty-five guys held on to the vision of winning."

Throughout the season, Bob nourished his team's vision of winning, and the use of imagination was how he did it. He repeatedly encouraged the players to see themselves and one another doing well. He urged them to visualize pitches, feel the connection of ball and bat, see runs being scored, hear the crowd cheering, smell the ballpark, and experience the joy of winning. And, at those crucial, final moments of the last game, as each player passed him going out onto the field, Bob had said, "See it happen! See it happen! Really *see* it!"

Obviously, they did.

In the Mind's Eye

Imagination played an enormous role during the "healing season" of my life—the year I faced cancer. Like a baseball team visualizing the specifics of winning games and coming out on top in the World Series, I visualized healing happening within me, in specific scenarios.

Many cancer patients are comfortable with the metaphor of "fighting" cancer, and they feel empowered by picturing healing happening in war-like ways. Others, instead of battling the disease and holding combat images in their minds, feel fortified by gentler approaches and imaginings. I was among that second group. While I did not wish to "fight" the disease, I was determined to "release" all the cancer cells from my body. So, several times each day, day-after-day, I played in my mind scenes that showed all the misguided cancer cells departing and my body becoming restored to radiant health and well-being.

Two of my visualizations were inspired by computer features.

The boxy old monitor I had back then, in 2000, had two buttons just below the screen. The one on the right said "power." The one on the left said "degauss." When I pressed the degauss button, a swirl of colors appeared on the screen. There were crackling sounds and the feeling of static electricity in front of the monitor. A moment later, all the colors, the cracklings, and the fuzzy feelings faded and disappeared.

I had heard that, in that "degauss" procedure, the monitor was releasing built-up, potentially-harmful electromagnetic energy. And, in fact, it seemed to me that, after degaussing, the space in front of and around the monitor did feel clearer, cleaner, and healthier.

I imagined that, like a computer, I too had a "degauss" button. Throughout the day, I imagined pressing my personal "degauss" button (in the middle of my forehead), which would release the negativity, toxicity, and aberrant cells—all "junk"—from my body that needed to be released... anything other than what served my health and wholeness.

I also imagined that, like the "refresh" feature on the top of the toolbar, I too had a "refresh" button (right over my heart). Likewise, throughout the day, I clicked on my personal "refresh" button and felt a sense of being new again: cleared and completely refreshed in the moment.

Another visualization I used was inspired by a simple, classic toy that many of us played with as children. Imprinted on a bright yellow piece of cardboard was a simple drawing of a smiling, hairless man. His face, along with some metal shavings, was covered by clear plastic. Using a magnet stick that was attached to the board with a string, I would lift and move the metal shavings onto the man's face to create a hair style, a beard, a moustache, and eye brows. Perhaps it was because I, too, was hairless that this toy came to mind.

The thought of it led to picturing a large magic wand being waved over me, from head to toe. The wand was held by a healing angel who visited me frequently to perform this procedure. It got so that I could practically feel her presence on my right side and see what was happening. As this angel extended her arm and passed the wand several feet above my body, the magnetic tip would draw to it everything that did not promote health and well-being.

Then the angel raised her arm, flicked the wand, and flung all the icky energies away from the tip into the heavens, where they were transformed and returned to Earth as wildflowers growing in a meadow. This visualization left me feeling as if all was right within my body and in the world.

The more I used these and other positive imaginings, the more healing scenarios came to me. In another playful one, I imagined that my immune cells were like life guards on patrol along ocean beaches. Wearing sunglasses, hats, and sunscreen to protect themselves, millions of these vigilant little cells sat on life guard stands throughout my body, watching their assigned areas and going to the rescue whenever needed.

When I visualized healing happening in these ways, I created calm and confidence in my mind and body. I felt certain that this, in turn, stimulated biological activities within me that promoted the healing process.

These healing visualizations have become like favorite old movies to me. I re-play them when I'm feeling stressed… whenever I want to release any kind of dis-ease and return to radiant health and well-being.

In addition to all the playful imaginings, I pictured test results reporting, "No evidence of cancer," which, at the end of treatment, is exactly what they said.

Two Doors Down

Although they were not yet engaged, Leah and Ben decided they were ready to build a partnership toward marriage. Consequently, Ben secured a new job in Leah's home town in Prescott and gave notice to his current employer. The couple agreed they were not ready to live together so Ben began to look for a place to rent in Prescott, and Leah joined him in the search.

Right from the start of that search, Leah found herself thinking, *Wouldn't it be nice if Ben found a place nearby me? Hmmm… wouldn't it be nice if Ben rented a house in the same development as me?*

Thinking such thoughts led to fantasies along those lines. For example, Leah pictured Ben walking his dog, Katy, from his house over to Leah's, and the three of them strolling along the tree-lined streets and playing in the neighborhood park together.

"The pictures in my mind got stronger and stronger," Leah said. "I imagined Ben and me taking turns tossing a ball to Katy. I saw Katy bounding back to us with the ball in her mouth and a look of delight in her eyes. I could practically smell her doggie breath on the ball. It felt so real."

One day Leah mused, *Wouldn't it be nice if Ben was living right in my cul-de-sac! Wow, we could easily have meals together, help each other, and get to know each other better so conveniently. I would LOVE that!*

And then she said out loud, "Wouldn't it be nice if Ben lived just two doors down from me?"

Along with picturing the dog walking, the playing in the park, and the meals together, Leah imagined Ben going in and coming out of the house two doors down from hers, on the left.

The very next morning, Leah came across a new rental listing in the online newspaper: "House for Rent. 3358 Curtis Street…" She thought, *Hey, that's my street. Near my number.* Immediately pushing herself away from the computer, she ran outside to check. It was the house just two doors down on the left!

Wow! This visualization stuff is really powerful! She thought. Ben agreed that the serendipity of it was amazing, and their vision just had to come to fruition.

However, when Ben called to inquire about the rental, he was told, "Pets are not allowed. No exceptions." Also, the rental offering was just for the summer, short-term, and unaffordable.

How can it be? Leah thought. *It seemed so perfect.* But, after struggling with some disappointment, she went back to the visualizations. She even repeated, *Wouldn't it be nice if Ben lived just two doors down from me?*

Another day passed. And another. On the third day after the disappointment, Leah spotted another new rental listing: "House for Rent. 3354 Curtis Street…" By that point Leah knew the numbers of all the houses in the cul-de-sac. Number 3354 was two doors down on the right!

Ben called immediately. This time he heard, "Dog? No problem." The lease time frame was flexible and the fee affordable. Everything fell into place with grace and ease. For the next six months, Ben lived two doors down from Leah. After that, they lived together in a new house, as husband and wife.

"Two doors down" has become a mantra for Leah and Ben, reminding them to visualize their dreams and then to surrender themselves to the outcome, with trust.

"Imagination is the preview of
life's coming attractions."

—ALBERT EINSTEIN

"Use your imagination not to scare yourself
to death, but to inspire yourself to life."

—ADELE BROOKMAN

"Inspiration comes from a level deeper than
thought. It comes when you are quiet: when
the mind is holding steady, the emotions are
calm, and the body is in balance. Then the
Soul comes forward with its joyfulness. When
it does, the imagination comes with it."

—JOHN-ROGER

"Be careful what you water your dreams with.
Water them with worry and fear and you will
produce weeds that choke the life from your
dream. Water them with love and optimism and
solutions and you will cultivate success. Always be
on the lookout for opportunities to turn a problem
into an opportunity for success. Always be on
the lookout for ways to nurture your dream."

—LAO-TZU

146

For Reflection, Journaling, and Discussion

1. What are you visualizing about your finances, your work, your home, your relationships, and your dreams?

2. Recall a time when you used imagination to inspire yourself and visualize success.

3. Into what situations and areas of your life would you like to now bring more positive imagination?

Reverence

May you appreciate the wonder that you are
and the miracle of all creation.

Sunshine Harbor

Every summer during my childhood, I spent time at my aunt and uncle's bungalow at the New Jersey shore. The bayside community was called "Sunshine Harbor." Everything about it seemed magical to me, including that name. From the time I arrived to the time I got back in the car to return to the city, except for church on Sundays, I ran about barefoot on what felt like holy ground.

During those summers, every once in while, one of the neighborhood kids would say, "Let's seine," and another kid would run off, get a seining net from his garage, and return to the beach.

Seining was a magnificent experience even when I simply watched. It was even better when I got to hold the pole on either end and drag the large net along the shoreline for awhile. We'd walk perhaps fifteen feet or so, unable to see what was below the surface of the water, unaware of what was being caught in the net. That activity, in and of itself, was wondrous.

Then, we'd experience the miracle of bringing the net to the shore and examining our "catch." Every time we did it, we saw a different variety of fish, jellyfish, seaweed, and baby crabs. So much LIFE! We would look at it all with awe and then return the net's rich contents to the sea where it quickly disappeared back into its home.

It struck me as a miracle that, whenever I looked at the water and saw only the surface, there were millions of life forms hidden in the depths.

Photo of the Day

About five years ago, my brother, Keith, started what he calls his "photo of the day" practice. It began when he had an epiphany. He realized that much time had passed in his life and he wondered, *Where did it go?*

Keith suddenly felt, in his own home on an ordinary day, at age forty-five, a deep appreciation for all the moments of his life so far. *So many have passed*, he thought. *So many forgotten.* And he wondered how many were ahead for him.

This wake-up call led Keith to take one photo each day, in a very purposeful way. His intention was to pause, savor a moment, and honor it by capturing it. While some of his photos immortalize beautiful sunsets, his garden in bloom, and his dogs in joyful play, many merely depict the seemingly mundane moments of life: a sunny-side-up egg frying in a pan, a just-poured glass of beer, and water flowing from the shower head.

"It's not about waiting for peak experiences or the high-point moments each day," said Keith. "I just want to stop and appreciate ordinary moments."

He explained that, now and then, he really "gets it," that there really are no ordinary moments. They're all magnificent. We don't usually see life this way unless some significant change shakes us up.

Recently, Keith and I talked about the Thornton Wilder play *Our Town*, and how the main character, Emily, deeply appreciates the simple routines of daily life after she dies giving birth and has the opportunity to go back and watch her own twelfth birthday. In fact, the blinding beauty that she sees in ordinary life is too much to bear. The way that Emily sees ordinary life from beyond the grave is a reminder to appreciate every moment.

Keith's "photo of the day" practice has given rise to the experience of reverence in him. He has cultivated the habit of always being watchful for simple-yet-sacred moments to capture. Because he is looking for them, he sees many more of them.

Jai Bhagwan

During the summer of 1990, my college-student daughter and I, along with a small group of men and women, attended a week-long program called "The Art of Joyful Living."

During our orientation, we learned that we would be using the greeting *Jai Bhagwan* before and after every session. Similar to *Namaste,* the greeting is said with palms together in the prayer position while bowing to one another.

At first, most of us mispronounced *Jai Bhagwan*... properly pronounced: Jai [rhymes with "eye"] Buh-GWAHN. And we bowed awkwardly.

Despite its beautiful meaning, which roughly translates to "The Light in me recognizes the Light in you," self-conscious chuckles accompanied our first *Jai Bhagwans.* By the third day, the giggles stopped.

We had all said *Jai Bhagwan* so often it had become comfortable and routine, like saying "hello" and "see you later."

During that week, we wrote, reflected, prayed, played, danced, made art, and shared stories with heart-centered telling and listening.

By the last day, with pretenses dropped and masks removed, everyone in the group was open and willing to be vulnerable… REAL. As a result, as we said our final good-byes, bows were graceful. The greeting was whispered. Eyes met with love… and with tears. A powerful feeling of awe filled each of us. It was an experience of respect beyond words… even beyond the word "reverence."

Jai Bhagwan, dear friend.

*"There are only two ways to live your life.
One is as though nothing is a miracle. The
other is as though everything is a miracle."*

—ALBERT EINSTEIN

*"There is only one valid way to partake of the
universe—whether the partaking is of food and
water, the love of another, or, indeed, a pill. That
way is characterized by reverence—a reverence
born of a felt sense of participation in the universe,
a kinship with all and with all matter."*

—DR. LARRY DOSSEY

*"People usually consider walking on water or thin
air a miracle. But I think the real miracle is…
to walk on earth. Everyday we are engaged in a
miracle which we don't even recognize: a blue sky,
while clouds, green leaves, the black curious eyes
of a child—our own two eyes. All is a miracle."*

—THICH NHAT HANH

*"There is no way of telling people that they
are all walking around shining like the
sun… the gate of heaven is everywhere."*

—THOMAS MERTON

For Reflection, Journaling, and Discussion

1. What do you remember from when you were a child, as you went about discovering the world around you?

2. What made you whisper, "Wow!"?

3. Back then, what stirred love, awe, joy, and well-being in you? A flitting butterfly? Snowflakes? Fireworks? Clouds? Swinging high and feeling one with the sky?

4. What stirs up such emotions now?

5. Recall a time when you caught a glimpse of the oneness of all creation. Consider writing about it, sharing it with someone close to you, or simply meditating upon the experience and its message to you.

6. Into what situations and areas of your life would you like to bring more reverence?

Wisdom

Guiding your way, wisdom will lead you
through knowledge to understanding.
May you hear its soft voice.

Polliwogs for Alaina

I felt like an excited parent on Christmas Eve as I lovingly spread an array of "tools" for the workshop participants across the top of a large oak table. The symbolic trinkets included feathers, stickers, stones, safety pins, pennies, and many more objects gathered from nature, a hardware store, and my home. At one end of the table I stacked a supply of zip-top bags to serve as "tool kits." Then, I covered it all with a large cloth so that the project would be hidden until it was time for the main activity.

I stepped back and surveyed the room. Everything was in place. But was I ready? My shaky knees warned me that I wasn't, not fully.

Normally, I feel completely relaxed at The Wellness Community, but that night I had the jitters. Instead of coming for group support, or to take an art class or other educational program, this time I was leading a workshop. As a grateful cancer survivor, I wanted to give something back. Something meaningful. Something *great*.

The door opened. Everyone was arriving. Whispering a quick prayer, I asked for just that: that the event be *great*.

My two-hour workshop, titled "Do What Makes YOU Strong," was designed to explore ways to tap into inner strength, and it concluded with a light-hearted, yet purposeful, activity. Each participant would assemble a personalized "tool kit" filled with various "tools" to take home for daily inspiration.

When I looked out into the eyes of cancer patients, survivors, and their loved ones, my heart opened and my knees steadied. The two hours passed quickly.

As participants said their goodbyes and started to leave, a young woman who had been sitting quietly in the back row approached me.

"I'm Alaina. And, I've got to tell you what happened tonight," she exclaimed, with her eyes big and bright. "When it was time to go to the activity table and gather items for our tool kits, I thought, *I wonder if she put a polliwog on that table.* For some crazy reason, I wanted a polliwog!"

Polliwog? I thought. *A tadpole?*

Reading my perplexed expression, Alaina laughed and said, "Oh, not a frog. A polliwog. You know, those seeds that come from maple trees. When I was little, my two sisters and I used to open them up and put them on our noses when they were fresh and sticky."

"Oh, helicopters!" I replied, picturing how I, too, had played with those seeds as a child.

"Yeah. When they got dry, we'd toss them in the air and watch them spin down. Sometimes we called them whirlybirds. But usually we called them polliwogs. I don't know why. But look, I've got three of them in my tool kit!" she declared with delight, shaking her see-through baggie.

How can this be? I thought. *I did not place any polliwogs on that table.*

Alaina went on to explain that, nearing the activity table, she felt both excitement and apprehension, wondering, *Why do I want a polliwog? What made me even think of a polliwog?*

"I didn't see it at first. Looking over all the stuff, I selected a bottle of bubbles, a pine cone, and one of the prayer print-outs. And, I kept thinking, *Of course there's no polliwog on this table!* But then, there it was, hardly visible, one little brown seed blending into the color of the oak table! It was lying between a puzzle piece and the pine cone I took. I was shocked. I picked it up and put it in my bag. Would you believe that, while I was returning to my seat, *two more* polliwogs appeared in my tool kit?!"

How can this be? I thought again. *I did not place any polliwogs on that table!*

Peering into Alaina's baggie, I recognized the source of the mystery polliwogs. Still tucked in between the brown ridges of the pine cone, I saw more of them. Seeds.

Even though the three boomerang-shaped seeds in Alaina's "tool kit" came out of a pine cone and not from a maple tree, they were an answer to prayer. And they offered guidance.

For both Alaina and me, those three seeds show-ing up the way they did seemed to be God saying, *I'm here and I hear you.*

Remembering how she and her two sisters had played freely and joyfully, Alaina felt led, by wisdom, to be childlike and trusting again, even while facing cancer.

And I realized that it's okay to release the habit of fretting over "being great." Greatness Itself is always present, making things great in ways I often can't see or even imagine. I also realized that all I have to do is prepare as best I can and then show up for presentations—for everything in life—with an open heart, a willingness to serve, and an attitude of surrender.

Alaina and the polliwogs remind me to listen carefully for the voice within, even if it seems strange or random or unnecessary. I heard that voice as I was driving away from my home, heading for the workshop. I felt an inner nudge to stop, get out of the car, and gather a collection of pine cones. There I was, stooping and slipping on the sloping ground beneath the pine trees, in order to pick up what I felt would be an adequate supply of pine cones. *I really need to be on my way to the center,* I thought. However, even though I had no idea why, I trusted that subtle inner prompting to gather those pine cones.

That simple-yet-wondrous experience with Alaina reminds me that wisdom "speaks" to us in many ways.

Move!

Just before my sixth chemotherapy treatment, when a friend suggested I read *It's Not about the Bike* by Lance Armstrong, I immediately felt two things. One was an inner certainty that the cancer survivor and Tour de France winner's book contained something I needed to know; the second was a sensation of being guided. Although I didn't hear any actual words, it *felt* as if someone was saying, *Get the book and read it.* And so I did, suspecting I would benefit from something Mr. Armstrong had to say about nutrition.

I began reading his story and continued along in a normal manner until I got to page 89, when suddenly one word on the bottom of that page made my body shiver. It was then that I knew what I needed to glean from this book. The word was "move."

"*Move*," Lance had said to himself. As long as he could move, he wouldn't be so sick, he told himself.

Immediately, I understood. *I* needed to "move."

For months, I had done many nourishing things for my body, mind, and spirit to cooperate with and to compensate for the chemotherapy. However, I had not exercised… at all. So, I added movement to my own healing "tool box." I started taking short walks and exercising gently in a swimming pool. When I did, my body responded with increased energy and a feeling of greater well-being.

That subtle feeling I had when I saw the word "move" was gentle, yet it clearly guided me toward additional self-care choices I could make in my recovery of wholeness, health, and well-being.

Inner GPS

I was on my way to a photo shoot for the "Gift of Courage" in *The Twelve Gifts of Birth* book. It was 10 A.M. on I-10 in Phoenix. Since it was well after the so-called "morning rush hour," when cars are barely moving, traffic was speeding along, above the posted limit. And, I was in the flow, driving too fast in a center lane. All of a sudden I heard... not with my ears... but *in* my body... the actual words, *Move over to the far right lane, NOW!*

The instruction seemed to originate in my heart and fill the trunk of my body in a way that was loud and clear, yet made no sound.

When I "received" those words, I knew I must heed them. Without giving them a thought, I calmly followed the inner directive. And then I wondered, *What was that all about?*

Moments later, my front right tire blew out. Being in the far right lane, I was able to quickly and easily get out of the flow of traffic, pull off the road, and come to a stop safely on the shoulder.

Three huge semi trucks then rumbled by. My little car shook in their wake.

I understood just how guided I had been. And I trembled with gratitude.

Turn Here

Before a book signing at a large chain store in Alabama, I arrived early with the intention to browse for new reading material for myself. As I stepped out from one of the aisles and turned around the end cap, I noticed a burly man with glistening eyes standing at the display where I would later be sitting. I approached and introduced myself as the author of the book he was clutching to his chest.

He stammered, "I'm… uh… Fred," and swallowed hard. At first I thought he felt embarrassed by his tears, but he went on to explain why he was so moved.

I learned that Fred had no intention of going to a bookstore that night. He was driving to another destination when he suddenly felt a perplexing urge to steer the car into the bookstore parking lot. With no particular objective, just trust in his heart, he followed the intuition and entered the store. A stack of copies of *The Twelve Gifts of Birth* displayed on a table right inside the front door caught his attention.

"I took a copy off the top, opened it, and started reading. I...," After a pause to regain composure, Fred went on.

"This is amazing. I... last night, I was driving my daughter to a friend's house," he said. "The subject of beauty came up... again. My daughter *is* beautiful. But she doesn't see it, because she doesn't look like the skinny models. She's built like me. She thinks she's ugly. I want to help her see her beauty. But I don't know how. "

His voice cracked. Again he paused.

"I... I was thinking about her when I felt that urge to turn into this parking lot."

Fred took a deep breath and shook his head. "Awesome, isn't it? How we're guided? I'm gonna keep trying to help her see her beauty. One thing I'm gonna do is give her a copy of this book. I like

how it tells her she was born with the gift of beauty.
And I'm gonna keep letting her know that I love her."
Awesome, isn't it? How we're guided?

Instead of Worry

In the summer of 2006, after observing an increase of fearful stories in the news and hearing many people express anxiety, my friend, Terri, shared a personal story via a mass email to her friends.

"When I was a little girl, my mom often told me that worrying doesn't do any good. Deep down we all know this is true, don't we?" she asked. "And yet, we often worry anyway."

And, she went on to explain how she let go of worry.

It was a few years earlier. Terri and her husband were worrying when their college-student daughter faced unexpected health challenges.

"Why are you worried about your daughter?" someone asked.

Terri was surprised at what seemed like an insensitive question and blurted out, "Because she has health challenges and that's what parents do... we worry about our children!"

That someone, whom Terri now refers to as an angel, gently said, "What would you say if I told you that when you worry about a loved one or anything else you are concerned about, you are sending negative energy to that person or situation?"

Terri said that that is the last thing she would ever want to do and "the angel" suggested trying something new.

"When you talk with your daughter on the phone, instead of asking about her headaches and chest pains, ask about her sorority meeting or chemistry lab. She may be in a happy state until your probing questions remind her of health concerns. And when you think of your daughter, see her surrounded with love and light, rainbows and bubbles. See her as a little girl helping you make chocolate chip cookies. In other words, *see and feel* happiness for your daughter."

Terri decided to try this new technique. For the next few days when she talked with her daughter on the phone, she asked only neutral questions. When she thought of her daughter throughout the day, she focused only on happy thoughts and memories.

Right away Terri noticed that she, herself, felt happier. Soon, her daughter noticed too and asked what her mom was doing differently. When Terri explained her conscious choice of positive thoughts and words, she was stunned when her daughter said, "Mom, for the last few days I've been feeling great!"

Within a short time, her daughter's health issues vanished.

That experience led Terri to practice "letting-go-of-worry" on a daily basis. Whenever she found herself thinking negative thoughts, she replaced those thoughts with positive ones. Soon, she found herself automatically focusing on the positive. She also observed more examples of how her thoughts often materialized.

Appreciating the sage advice given to her by that "angel" acquaintance, Terri felt a nudge to pass that advice on to others in the form of her story.

I am feeling nudged to pass this "angel" wisdom on to you and to share more about how I use this touchstone.

Soon after reading Terri's email, I came across two photos that help me to see my own daughters in the way recommended by Terri's angel. One photo captures my older daughter in midair, as she is jumping into a pool. Her face and body radiate joy, freedom, health, gratitude... all the highest energies and life's gifts. Similarly, the second photo demonstrates this state of being in my younger daughter as she beams with delight as we are entering Disney World for the first time.

When any of our loved ones face a challenge, we can try to hold them in our minds and hearts in this way, picturing them at their very best, with life's gifts flowing through them.

Certainly, although it is wiser than worrying, there are many times when it is easier to say this than do this.

Just as I completed this touchstone example, I got word that my cousin's four-year-old grandson will be having surgery on the optic nerve. At age two he was diagnosed with neurofibromatosis, a disease that causes tumors to grow along the body's nervous system, in the brain, and on the spinal cord. This sweet little boy has already had major surgery to remove a tumor at the base of his skull. He recovered very well from that surgery and I pray that he does from this next one, too.

I am intending, as best I can, to refrain from worrying and feeling sorry for him and from asking, "Why?" But I can understand how those closest to him might find it nearly impossible not to worry at all or to question. (I may slip and do some of that, too.)

I'm holding an image of him, in my mind and heart, with delight in his eyes, joy in his smile, and health throughout his body.

Wisdom

Please join me in picturing all our loved ones, all the "children" of the world—you and me, too—radiating health, happiness, and well-being. May we be guided by wisdom.

Touchstones

"There are no mistakes, no coincidences. All
events are blessings given to us to learn from."
—ELISABETH KÜBLER-ROSS

"As you rest from all worry, you are
preparing the way for renewal."
—THE DAILY WORD

"Life can only be understood backwards,
but it must be lived forwards."
—SØREN KIERKEGAARD

"To know how to choose a path with heart is
to learn how to follow intuitive feelings."
—JEAN SHINODA BOLEN

For Reflection, Journaling, and Discussion

1. Recall a time when you experienced being led to go in a certain direction or make a particular choice. How did you experience that inner guidance? Was it through a voice? A sensation in your body? An image in your mind's eye? A spontaneous knowing that popped into your awareness?

2. How did you respond to the guidance?

3. In what other ways do you experience the gift of wisdom? (For example, in dreams, song lyrics, synchronistic encounters with people, insights shared by others, book passages, seeming "coincidences," etc.)

4. Into what situations and areas of your life would you like to bring more wisdom?

Love

It will grow each time you give it away.

Four-leaf Clover

It was August 18, 1999, back near the start of the Polished Stone Tour. My husband and I were in Portland, Oregon, at a center for children with special needs.

After receiving a polished stone from me, a bright-eyed young boy, Michael, reached into his pocket, retrieved something, and held it hidden in his closed fist.

"Now I want to give *you* something," he smiled, extending his hand to me. "It's for luck. I found it this morning."

I opened my palm. Onto it he dropped something moist and green. For a second I felt confused. But then I recognized it as a clover that, indeed, had four leaves on just one stem.

I got a quick flash-back to when my cousin, John, and I looked for four-leaf clovers when we were about the same age as Michael. We'd search through patches of clover at our grandparents' house for hours. When we tired of the quest, we would each "make" a four-leaf clover by combining a regular three-leaf clover with a stem from which two of the leafs had been removed. We held the two stems together just so and tried to make the combo look like a true four-leaf clover. We never did find a real one.

I told Michael that I greatly appreciated his gesture, that I would enjoy holding his clover for the rest of my visit there, and that I would certainly take the memory of it with me. However, I did not want to take the actual clover with me; I wanted him to keep it for himself.

"Why?" he asked.

"Four-leaf clovers are rare and hard to find," I answered. "I used to look for them a lot and I never found one."

"Really?" he said.

Love

"Really," I said, and went on to tell him about how I created those look-a-likes.

"Then for sure I want you to have this real one," said Michael. "I find them all the time. Don't worry. I'll find another one."

I marveled at the pureness of his loving. And I was struck by the symbolism. For Michael, those four-leafed clovers were like love. He gave plenty away and always found plenty more.

Love Is a Decision

"*L*ove is a decision."

When I first heard that expression at a Marriage Encounter Weekend almost forty years ago, I bristled. *A decision? How unromantic!* I was a young wife then, in my twenties, with a lot to learn about love and marriage. By the end of the weekend, I was willing to embrace the concept. However, it wasn't until months later that I "got it" on a deeply personal level.

It was a winter morning. Overnight, a few inches of fresh snow had fallen upon a layer of packed snow and ice. During breakfast, my husband, Frank, and I argued over something. He stormed out the door. I felt hurt and angry. I knew he did, too.

From the kitchen window, fuming with self-righteousness, I watched him struggle to get the car to move up the incline of our driveway, and out onto the road. He repeatedly shoveled, sprinkled sand around all the tires, and tried rocking the car out of its stuck position. The wheels spun, but the car wouldn't budge.

I see it as funny, now, how the car reflected our stuckness!

Back to then... After a few minutes, I remembered: *I have a choice here. Stay angry? Or decide to love?*

The choice was clear. Deciding to act in a loving way, even though I didn't yet *feel* the emotion, I thrust my bare feet into my snow boots by the front door, yanked my long wool coat off its hook, pulled it on over my flannel nightwear, and padded over to our detached garage. By the time I reached my husband, the ice around my heart was beginning to melt. A trickle of love came forth. Despite the outer cold, I could feel myself getting warmer on the inside.

I got in the driver's seat and pressed gently on the gas, while Frank pushed from behind the car. Perhaps, like the ice around our hearts, the frozen snow beneath the tires had melted. In any event, with grace and ease, the wheels turned and carried the car up the incline. When the car was situated on the snowplowed street, I shifted the gear into park. Frank opened the door and extended his hand to help me out. I accepted it with mine and let him pull me into a warm embrace before he drove off to work.

That morning, I "got it." Not just in my head, but in my heart… in my whole body, in fact. With the warmth of love flowing freely by that point, I felt uplifted and energized for the rest of the day.

It's not always that easy. But it is simple. We can decide to love.

The Demo Lady

Sheila is a food "demo" lady at a popular, specialty grocery store.

"I don't know why or how this happens," Sheila said. "But, when I'm at work, no matter what people look like or how they act, I see beyond that to something I can't put into words. And, I simply love them! Everyone!"

Watching Sheila's eyes sparkle as she spoke of this, I thought, *Sheila is really an "unconditional love" demo lady.*

As she described her experiences to me, she exuded love. Love flowed outward from her, into the world. And I felt touched, not just by her enthusiastic loving, but by Love itself.

Father Judge

I never met Father Mychal Judge. However, I feel as though I knew him. In a very real way, I do know the spirit of him. He was a Franciscan friar and priest—and a graduate of St. Bonaventure University, as am I. He received his B.A. in 1957, ten years before I entered that Franciscan university as a freshman.

I learned about Father Judge when I heard about his death on 9/11, first in an email from my alma mater, and later in news stories. It wasn't until I watched the film, *Saint of 9/11*, that this man's story became a touchstone for me.

The gold standard he reflects to me is not related to how he died on that day in service as chaplain for the Fire Department of New York City. Rather, it is how he lived, each and every day: loving all humanity. He ministered to the homeless, recovering addicts, people with AIDS, gays and lesbians—all the brothers and sisters among us who have been alienated in any way. Day by day, Father Judge helped people see the dignity that is within them, despite all outer appearances. Day by day, he lived "in love" and gave love away.

For example, in the 1980s, during the height of fear about AIDS, when many AIDS patients were isolated and felt rejected, instead of avoiding contact with them, Father Judge worked with them face-to-face, without wearing a mask. To further show his acceptance, caring, and respect, he massaged their feet with holy oil. When one particular dying man asked, "Do you think God hates me?" Mychal Judge answered by lifting the frail man, rocking him in his arms, and kissing the top of his head.

A hospital worker who observed this said, "Father Mychal stood in for God and restored that man's worth."

Aren't we all called to do this? At times? Stand in for God? Restore worth to someone? With love?

The Presence of Love

One day, while I was a student at the University of Santa Monica, I was in the passenger seat of a car going west. A classmate was driving and we were stopped at a light on Wilshire Boulevard. The Pacific Ocean was in sight, just a few blocks ahead.

Suddenly, the sunlight seemed to take on deeper beauty, more clarity, and a new quality. It was not just that the noonday sun shone in the sky and provided bright light. It was as if light was an actual *presence* all around us. In that moment I suddenly felt both "within Light" and "within Love." Love seemed to be a living substance, present everywhere and in everything, including me.

I noticed the distinction between loving my family, my friends, the beautiful day, being in California—loving people and things—and simply loving… experiencing love as a fundamental state of being. In that moment love washed over me, into me, through me, and out to everything, without restriction. I *was* love.

Although that wave of loving lasted just a moment, it left an impression on me—an indelible mark that I can draw on for the rest of my life. Sometimes, when I feel alone and separate, I close my eyes, breathe deeply, and recall this visceral experience. And then I simply trust that, no matter where I am or how I am feeling, I'm always in the presence of Love.

We all are.

Love

*"Your task is not to seek for love, but merely
to seek and find all of the barriers within
yourself that you have built against it."*
—FROM *A COURSE IN MIRACLES*

"Man loves because he is Love."
—EKNATH EASWARAN

*"Love is not something you feel.
It is something you do."*
—DAVID WILKERSON

"Where there is great love there are always miracles."
—WILLA CATHER

"Love heals."
—THE BUDDHA

For Reflection, Journaling, and Discussion

1. Recall a time when you made a decision to love, despite feeling unloving.

2. Recall an example of seeing love expressed in a gesture by someone else, either toward you or toward another person. How did witnessing that affect you?

3. Who comes to mind when you look for an example of someone who seems to simply exude love? This may be either a real person or a fictional character.

4. Into what areas of your life would you like to bring more loving?

Faith

May you believe.

Granny's Barbeque

One spring morning on The Polished Stone Tour, my husband and I turned off the main highway and meandered through Texas countryside for an hour or so. We decided to let back roads lead us where they may. As we neared a small town, a handmade sign invited us to lunch at Granny's Barbeque. A second, third, and fourth sign directed the way. We followed the signs. Arriving early for the mid-day meal, we were the only two customers in the establishment.

After serving us heaping plates of barbeque and tall glasses of iced tea, Granny sat down at the table next to us and chatted while she waited for other customers to arrive. When twenty minutes passed and no one else entered, Granny rose and joined us at our table.

Sharing stories, we learned that Granny was a retired schoolteacher who loved to cook. She had opened her restaurant just a week ago. We described our tour, where we had been so far, and where we were headed.

We appreciated her food and hospitality. So before driving off, I fetched a copy of *The Twelve Gifts of Birth* from the RV and gave it to Granny. She asked us to remain a few more minutes, while she looked through it. We sat together again as she read the book. Slowly, she considered each gift and commented.

"Ah, yes... This is true... Praise the Lord... Amen... Ah-huh... Yesiree."

Granny made an affirmative comment after each gift. Until faith. "No," she said, choking back tears. "Not everyone has this one. Not my husband."

We stayed at that table for quite some time, talking about faith. What is faith? What does it encompass? What do we believe? What principles do we live by?

At the end of our discussion, Granny was still concerned because her husband did not share her religious beliefs. But we agreed that faith is both about God and not about God. We agreed that faith transcends religion. And we agreed that "faith is being sure of what we hope for and certain of what we do not see" (Heb. 11:1).

By Any Other Name

Ann, Anna, Annie, Mom, Mother, Aunt Anna, Aunt Annie, Nana, Mrs. Gorda…

Over the years, my mom was called by all of these names and a few more. Her given name was "Anna Victoria." My dad's affectionate name for her was "Anutie."

All these names were used during the calling hours before my mom's funeral as people "paid their respects" in the form of storytelling. I especially appreciated anecdotes told by my mom's early childhood friends and co-workers at the telephone company because they offered new insights and glimpses of the woman who had given birth to me.

After reminiscing with family members and friends, I realized how every single one of us who was in relationship with the legally named "Anna

Victoria" had a unique perspective about her. And, not one of us knew her completely.

We don't know anyone completely. We don't even know ourselves completely. We are all, in large part, a mystery.

I thought about all this during my mom's funeral Mass.

Suddenly I felt deep appreciation for how every person on the planet has his and her own unique relationship with the Mystery that goes by the name of God... and by other names... and is beyond all names... in which I have faith.

My One-Day Friend

In spite of needing to have four impacted wisdom teeth removed, my spirits were high as I was admitted to the hospital. I expected to read, relax, and watch TV before and after the surgery—luxuries for a mother with two active toddlers. I also looked forward to ordering from a menu and being able to eat meals—even hospital food—without having to prepare those meals or clean up afterward. I recalled my five-day maternity stays and pictured something similar.

Yes, I was naïve and immature to anticipate a vacation-like atmosphere. But, I was only twenty-four years old. And the year was 1973. Back then, hospitalization for minor surgery, with a multi-day recovery stay, was standard.

208

Crossing the threshold of room 425, my heart sank. I tried to conceal my dismay when the so obviously ill, older woman in the far bed rasped, "Hello, dear."

Sparse graying-blond hairs poked out wildly from her head. Her emaciated body seemed lost in the bed. Her pale yet friendly blue eyes and prominent cheek bones suggested that she had been a very attractive woman. I suspected that the physical beauty that had once been hers had been worn away by cancer and its treatments.

At the time, I was so afraid of cancer that I could barely speak the word. Just a subtle reference to the disease would cause my knees to weaken and my throat to tighten. It was unsettling to think that I was going to be in such close proximity to serious illness.

Her parched lips broke into a smile as she repeated, "Hello, dear. I'm Mrs. Cougan."

I felt as if I had been plunged into ice water. Recovering a little from feelings of shock and fear, I introduced myself and proceeded to get settled into my side of the room.

Then I left the room to find ways to pass the time. First, I visited a young mother whom I had met in pre-admission. Like me, that woman was scheduled for a minor surgery. During the pre-admission process, we had hoped that we would be roommates and joked about ordering pizza. While spending time with her, I again felt disappointment with my room assignment.

After leaving her room, I walked the halls and came upon the chapel. I entered and sat alone in the silence. Then I began to reproach myself for what I saw as silly and unrealistic expectations, for thinking so much of myself and so little for others, and for running away from the reality in my room. I decided to drop my expectations and try to change my perspective.

So I returned to room 425 and walked toward Mrs. Cougan, cautiously. Since she was facing the blank wall, with her back toward me, I tiptoed around the foot of her bed and peaked to see if she was asleep or awake. Her eyes were open.

"Oh, hello dear. You're back," she said, seeming glad to see me.

I asked if I could visit with her for a few minutes. In a warm and welcoming way, she nodded her head toward the chair near her pillow. Sitting close to her, I saw something powerful in Mrs. Cougan's eyes. Peace? Yes. And a kind of knowing.

I learned that Mrs. Cougan had no children, that we attended the same church, and that we shared a love for flowers. Our discussion then moved beyond small talk to personal matters and beliefs about life. Perhaps since she knew her time was limited, she wasted none of it hiding behind a mask. I soon felt a fondness for Mrs. Cougan and sensed a special bond between us, like a mother-daughter relationship. We had never met before, yet I felt as if we had.

After freshening myself before the nighttime visiting hours, knowing my husband would come by, I offered to help Mrs. Cougan with any grooming she would like to do, as her husband would be coming too. She asked me to comb her hair and place a drop of rosewater on her wrist.

Visiting hours came and went. Mrs. Cougan and I talked some more. Then a nurse gave me something to help me sleep.

When I woke at dawn, I was anesthetized for surgery. After the procedure, I didn't regain consciousness until late afternoon. And then it was dim. In fact, for the remainder of my hospital stay, I was in a state of fog and pain. No reading, no TV, no eating, no more talking.

Two days later, it was time for me to be discharged and to say good-bye to Mrs. Cougan. I found that hard to do. Just as I had first felt reluctant to walk toward her, after sharing that room with Mrs. Cougan, I felt reluctant to walk away from her.

Leaving the hospital, I promised myself that I would visit and bring a pretty poster to tape on to the blank wall she faced half the day. However, as days passed and I was once again immersed in homemaking and child care, thoughts of Mrs. Cougan faded away.

A week or so later, I remembered Mrs. Cougan. Even though I had not yet purchased a poster for her wall, I arranged for child care so I could visit her the following day. *I'll just bring myself*, I thought. I went to bed that night looking forward to seeing her.

About 11 P.M., as I was drifting into sleep, a strange disorientation came over me. For a moment I felt uncomfortable stretching sensations in my body, like I was being pulled and elongated. I had never felt anything like it. Frightened, I woke my husband. As I tried to describe what I was experiencing, suddenly I had an intuition.

"Mrs. Cougan is dying," I said. I felt absolutely certain of it.

My husband sat up and tried to comfort me. We talked for a while before saying good night. My husband fell back to sleep quickly, but I was wide awake.

Then another unusual experience came upon me.

It began with a sense of warmth around me and within me. I felt bathed in a sweet, soft calm. The calm grew into a state of bliss. I got out of bed, walked to our living room, and sat on our sofa. There I stayed. For more than an hour, I simply sat and savored a feeling of deep peace, love, and joy.

The following morning, I could hardly believe what had happened. In fact, I doubted the whole thing. I told myself that it must have been some sort of delayed reaction to the anesthesia and pain medication.

However, a call to the hospital confirmed that, indeed, Mrs. Cougan had died the night before, at the time I had "known" of it. I felt baffled and awed.

Three months later, my grandmother suffered a stroke while she was in that same hospital for tests. I sat outside the intensive care unit, waiting for other family members to arrive. As I was counting down the minutes until I could see my grandmother and worrying that she might die, Mrs. Cougan "appeared" in my consciousness.

For a few moments I could see with a kind of double vision. My eyes perceived the table where I sat, the chairs at the table, other people in the room, and the drink-dispensing machines.

And, somehow, I could also "see" Mrs. Cougan. It was as if she was behind a scrim or a veil very close to me, in front of all the other physical objects and people in the room.

The woman I saw looked beautiful and healthy, with a full head of gleaming blond hair and blue eyes restored to deep color. Light radiated within her, outward from her, and all around her. She was made of light.

Her lips didn't move, but I clearly "heard" Mrs. Cougan say, "Yes, your grandmother is going to die, dear. But do not be afraid. Look at me. Death is a beginning."

I felt stunned... and completely assured.

My grandmother did die. Three days later. Although I felt sadness for the loss of her physical presence, I imagined my grandmother, like Mrs. Cougan, shining with light.

Now and then, I reach for the memory of this post-death visit from my one-day friend. And I see Mrs. Cougan, my grandmothers, my mother, and my father... all my departed loved ones... shining with light.

Arthur and the Butterfly

I met Andrea when our paths crossed at a grief conference called "When a Child Dies" at which I had been asked to speak about *The Twelve Gifts*. Literally, Andrea and I bumped into each other as we both approached a display of photos. After exchanging "excuse-mes" and introductions, Andrea led me to the area where her son's photos were featured.

"This is my miracle boy," she said, tenderly touching a picture of her son, Arthur, taken on his eleventh birthday, shortly before he died. Leaning in to see that photo, what I most noticed was a pair of brilliant and expressive blue eyes. Later that day, in a sharing workshop and in conversations that followed, I learned why Andrea called Arthur her "miracle boy."

After a normal and easy pregnancy, Arthur was born at 8:15 A.M. on October 5, 1993, at an army hospital. "Holding my newborn son, I experienced perfect peace," she said. "It was as if everything was right in this world, even though military helicopters were hovering outside the nursery window and the Gulf War was raging on the other side of the world."

Andrea didn't worry that her son displayed weak suckling or that his cries were quieter than those of all the other screaming newborns. As weeks passed, although Arthur was not meeting the milestones outlined in all the parenting books, Andrea trusted the caveat phrase that appeared in all those books: "Of course, your child could be different."

He's just progressing at his own rate, Andrea assured herself.

But at the four-month mark, Arthur was diagnosed with infantile spasms and Andrea was told 95 percent of all babies born with this condition will be profoundly retarded and disabled.

Not Arthur, thought Andrea. *He will be in the 5 percent.*

"I was determined to 'fix' him," Andrea said and described myriad treatments suggested by specialists and performed by her and a team of volunteers. But, instead of showing signs of improvement, Arthur got weaker and weaker. When blood appeared in his stools and Arthur was hospitalized, the doctor said, "He's not going to live long; I advise you to take him home and just love him." Andrea and her husband agreed and did just that. Abandoning the special diet and physical therapy, they simply cuddled, cooed, and loved Arthur, while waiting for him to die.

After weeks of sleeping nearly twenty-four hours each day, Arthur suddenly "woke up." Slowly, day by day, he became more aware. He was not thriving—he still could not hold his head up on his own—but he was surviving. Clearly, he was not ready to die. Praying for guidance, Andrea continued to look for the treatment that would "fix" Arthur.

One day, when Arthur was three years old, after asking God over and over again, "Why, why, why aren't you helping him?!" Andrea received an answer in the lyrics of a song on the car radio. Hearing the words, "God doesn't have grandchildren," Andrea suddenly shifted into the perfect peace she had felt when she had first held Arthur in the hospital nursery.

"I understood immediately that Arthur was perfect *just the way he was*. He was on his own life course, in his own relationship with God. I'm not in charge here, and there is nothing to fix."

Even though Arthur had no muscle tone, even though doctors did not know for sure what he saw and heard and experienced inside himself, Andrea knew for sure that there was intelligence, wisdom, love, and beauty in Arthur's body and consciousness. Those around him could easily tell from his expressions and sounds when he was happy and when he was not.

"He definitely showed joy," Andrea said. "Lots of joy. Often at night we would hear him laughing, and we wondered, 'What is he experiencing? Is he visiting with angels?'"

According to a Yaqui holy man, that's exactly what he was doing.

When Arthur was four years old, Andrea heard about a Native American holy man and healer who lived on a nearby reservation. The Yaqui elder was well respected as a shaman by his people and happened to be a friend of a friend. Eager to learn as much as she could about how Arthur experienced life, Andrea arranged for the shaman to come and visit her son.

While communicating with Arthur, the shaman had a convulsive seizure. Coming out of that, the shaman explained that, although Arthur's outside world seemed small, his inside world was vast and rich. Andrea had been concerned that Arthur was bored. "He is definitely not bored," the shaman assured her. "Inside he is living fully, visiting with Spirit. Meeting him has been a great gift to me," the shaman said. And he explained further to Andrea, "He is here because he loves you. He is here in service to you."

"That humbled me," said Andrea. "What that shaman said. Arthur in service to *me*? I thought that, as his mother, *I* was in service to *him*. What the shaman said—and the many miracles that happened during Arthur's life—led me to thinking differently about all my relationships. Might we *all* be in service to one another?"

One year passed. And another. And another. During the next *seven* years, Andrea heard, several more times, "He is not going to live long." Yet, again and again, Arthur surprised everyone and recovered from what had looked like a near-death episode.

"During those years, Arthur taught me so many amazing things," said Andrea. "Such as the importance of being real and telling the truth. He had a way of reading people. Whenever we were with someone who was fibbing or exaggerating, Arthur would laugh in a certain way. My friends called him a 'BS Meter.'"

Arthur died while sleeping peacefully at 5:18 A.M. on December 9, 2004, two months after his eleventh birthday. Andrea noted the matching numbers of his birth and death: 8:15 and 5:18. "Arthur's whole life was filled with mysteries and miracles," she said. "And they continue.

"I miss him and I wish he was still here, physically," Andrea added. "But I sense him often. For example, at my work as a registered nurse one day, while helping a child with cerebral palsy, I distinctly heard Arthur say, 'Mom, take care of *these kids*.' That led me to go back to school so I could advance beyond RN and become a nurse practitioner. I also chose to specialize, as Arthur urged, in working with special needs children.

"Another time, I was hiking the floor of the Grand Canyon. At one point, to rest a bit, I laid on top of a vacant picnic table, closed my eyes, and talked to Arthur, as I so often do. Then I fell asleep. When I woke, I noticed a butterfly resting nearby on my back pack. I tried to shoo it off, but it would not move. Finally I knocked it off and it fell to the ground. It looked lifeless. Reaching for it, however, I saw that it was not dead, just kind of floppy. Like Arthur. Then, the butterfly flew to my boot and stayed there. Amazingly, that butterfly accompanied me for almost a mile, while I walked. Was that Arthur?

Had Arthur somehow sent it to me? I don't know." Her voice quivered then gained strength.

"This I *do* know," Andrea continued. "Life is a wondrous mystery. And having Arthur was the most wonderful, beautiful, magical, blessed experience of my life."

I was—*I am*—so inspired by this woman who experienced the loss of her son, yet still has so much faith in the beauty and miraculousness of life.

Yes, babies are born with special needs. Children die. Accidents happen. Sometimes horrific things happen. Life here on earth can be confusing and painful. And yet, there is so much goodness. We can see life's gifts at work in our lives. Miracles happen. Life is a miracle. There is order in the Universe.

May we believe.

*"The most important question a person can
ask is, 'Is the Universe a friendly place?'"*

—ALBERT EINSTEIN

*"Be not afraid of life. Believe that life is worth
living and your belief will help create the fact."*

—WILLIAM JAMES

*"Truly I tell you, if you have faith as small as
a mustard seed, you can say to this mountain,
'Move from here to here,' and it will move.
Nothing will be impossible for you."*

—LUKE 17:20

The Universe is unfolding as it should.
Therefore be at peace with God,
Whatever you conceive Him to be...
With all its sham, drudgery, and broken dreams,
It is still a beautiful world.
Strive to be happy.

—FROM DESIDERATA BY MAX EHRMANN

For Reflection, Journaling, and Discussion

1. What is your foundational belief about the world?

2. Recall a time when you took a "leap of faith," a time that required faith in order for you to go forward. What were the results? What did you learn from that experience?

3. Recall a time when you changed a belief and experienced greater peace as a result.

4. Into what situations and areas of your life would you like to now bring more faith?

Afterword

Dear Gifted One,

Thank you for reading this book. I hope these touchstone stories have reminded you of the gifts that dwell within you. I also hope that these stories, along with others that you collect from your own experience, will inspire you to use your gifts more and more, day by day, bringing their power into all the areas of your life and into the world for the greater good.

Before completing this book, I want to share one last touchstone story. It is a dream I had while I was in treatment for lymphoma.

In the dream, I was observing the happenings inside my body. The view I had was of a brightly colored, animated film, not a realistic, scientific depiction. I watched as a Disney-like story unfolded.

The first thing I saw was a long line of ivory-toned cells resting against a red wall. I understood them to be immune cells. Each cell was a unique character, with a face and a personality. Each wore a hat, pulled down low over closed eyes.

As my view expanded, I saw hundreds of these sweet little cells dozing side-by-side throughout the walls of my arteries and veins. All was quiet, like a children's nap time.

One cell stirred, stretched, and opened his eyes. A second cell followed, while the remainder of them continued to sleep.

Those two awakened cells suddenly became aware of a danger around them and showed concern. They tried to wake other cells, but none responded. The expressions on those two cells suggested that they felt small, helpless, and sad.

Somehow, in a flash, the two waking cells became strengthened. Resembling unlikely heroes in a children's adventure story, the two little guys expanded with determination. Clearly, they wanted to save the kingdom and restore the good!

But, as they surveyed the apathy around them and felt the magnitude of the threat, they shrunk back. "What can *we* do?" they said to each other. "Maybe we should just go back to sleep."

After a pause, they shook their heads and said, "*No!* We must stay awake!"

Then, they looked up and noticed *me*. I felt enormous love and caring from those two brave little cells. And, I loved them back. As love flowed between us, a light appeared inside them. They began to glow.

Stirred by the broadcasted light, a nearby cell opened his eyes, saw the two cells glowing, and also became bright. This happened with another cell. Then another. And another. My body started to fill with more and more light as all the immune cells woke up, looked around, and began to glow. Along with light, my body felt filled with love.

The scene inside my body ended there, but the dream continued.

Feeling a sensation of lifting out of my body, I hovered for a moment over my bed. Then, I floated beyond the walls of my house and traveled around my neighborhood, which was completely dark and still, with everyone asleep.

Suddenly, one light blinked on. Then, another. And another. One by one by one, many lights blinked on. They were not streetlights or lamps in houses. Rather, each luminary was a person, waking up and becoming brighter, just as my cells had done. I rose higher. Moving over the land, I saw an expanse of twinkling lights sparking everywhere. Suddenly there was a great burst of light and the entire Earth, as far as I could see, glowed with a peaceful radiance.

I woke up from that dream feeling healed and hopeful for the future of humanity.

Consider how we *are* like cells in a body: seemingly separate and small, and yet connected, a part of the whole. *And*, we are each filled with tremendous power.

Now, yes, there is confusion in the world. There is confusion in each of us. And, yes, we face challenges. Sometimes our personal challenges and challenges in the world seem too big to solve. At times, we feel small and helpless. Sometimes, we even feel doomed.

However, as the French philosopher, scientist, and Jesuit priest, Teilhard de Chardin once said, "The day will come when, after harnessing the ether, the winds, the tides, and gravitation, we shall harness for God the energies of love. And, on that day for the second time in the history of the world, man will have discovered fire."

I believe with Teilhard de Chardin. I believe within us there is the enormous energy of love that makes it possible for us to handle whatever comes our way. And, I believe that strength, beauty, courage, compassion, hope, joy, talent, imagination, reverence, wisdom, faith—*all of life's gifts*—are "energies of Love." When we harness these energies, it will be like discovering fire all over again.

For the most part, though, we haven't yet fully realized the power in us, the wealth, our true value. However, there is a groundswell of growing consciousness among us.

Have you ever seen the 1977 science fiction film, *Close Encounters of the Third Kind*? The main character, Roy, who is played by Richard Dreyfuss, has a vague image of a mountain in his mind after he sees a UFO. Feeling compelled to find the meaning of the image, he attempts to form that mountain in a pile of shaving cream in his hand, in a heap of mashed potatoes on his dinner plate, in mounds of sand outdoors, and in some soil he carts into his kitchen. With each zealous effort, he exclaims, "This means something! This means something!"

Sometimes I feel like Roy. Often, when I think about, speak about, or write about The Twelve Gifts, my heart seems to proclaim, "This means something! This means something... *something much more than we yet realize!*" I want to know: What is it about these gifts that we do not yet realize? I am always on the lookout, in my experiences and in others, for deeper understandings of The Twelve Gifts.

I sense that when we *do* realize (as in, truly understand the power of these gifts), we are going to realize (as in, bring about) a profound transformation, within ourselves and on Earth. I also sense that, even with the deep appreciation I have for life's gifts, it is only the tip of the iceberg of what is possible for me, for all of us, to realize. Perhaps that's why, like Roy, I feel driven to seek better understanding… to really "get it" as a reader in Boston, Susan, said to me.

"After reading the message of *The Twelve Gifts of Birth,* I get it," Susan said. "But how do I *really 'get it'*?"

I invite you, again, to join me on the quest for *realizing* life's gifts, for *really "getting it."* Please join me and Susan, as well as Mazi, Heather, Zoey, Penny, Olivia, Jack, Margaret, Kathy, Nancy, Kay, Betsy, Leah, Ben, Keith, Alaina, Terri, Fred, Sheila, Michael, Granny, Andrea, and the hundreds of thousands—millions—of others who are seeking to remember, recognize, and realize who we really are.

Along with collecting and recalling our inspirational stories, we can use prayers, quotes, affirmations, music, metaphors, symbols, rituals, and many other activities to help us access our gifts. Visit www.charlenecostanzo.com to explore various

233

touchstone tools and techniques. Sign up there to receive *Today's Touchstone*.

My wish for all of us? May we remember: One by one and day by day, that by using life's gifts, we can increase health, harmony, and wholeness in our bodies, in our relationships, in our finances, in our homes, in our work, in our communities, and in the world.

With love, blessings, and best wishes,

Charlene

Visual Touchstones

Pictures Worth a Thousand Words

Black-and-white line drawings appear on the first page of each chapter, along with the name of the gift that is the chapter's focus. Each is a miniature of a drawing that kids can color in to help them learn about and reflect on The Twelve Gifts. The full-size coloring pages, created by graphic artist Nathan Arnone, can be found at www.charlenecostanzo.com, under "Tips and Tools." Thank you, Nathan.

And, thank you, Jill Reger, for the photographs that inspired these coloring pages. Jill's hand-tinted photographs of scenes that reflect The Twelve Gifts appear in *The Twelve Gifts of Birth* book.

The Twelve Gifts Symbols

You may have noticed that twelve simple signs, or icons, are used in this book, at the end of each story. Each sign is a symbol for a particular gift. The following legend offers some insights into the gifts and their corresponding symbols:

Strength

Strength is in the foundation of who we are. It helps us to survive. Strength is not only physical but is also manifested by will, resolve, determination, and perseverance. With strength, we do the right thing—and admit we're wrong when we don't. We draw on strength in many ways, and when we use it, we increase it. A triangle is a good symbol of strength because it has a strong base and foundation.

Beauty

Each of us has the capacity to experience beauty in the world around us, and we all have beauty within us. Sometimes beauty is obvious. Sometimes it is hidden. But we can always look for it and find it. Appreciating beauty in all its forms and bringing it forth from within ourselves can greatly enrich our lives. A flower is a universally recognized symbol for beauty.

Courage

Courage is often associated with bravery and heroic acts. But we all tap into courage every day in small, seemingly ordinary ways. All of us are called to be heroes. Maybe, most importantly, to be true to ourselves, we need courage. The spiral is a symbol of each person's own path and the courage that it takes to follow it.

Compassion

When we understand and care about how another person feels, that's compassion. Compassion involves not only feelings, or empathy, but also actions, like taking steps to relieve the suffering of others. Sometimes compassion involves forgiveness. We must be compassionate not only to other people but also to ourselves. The rain drop or tear drop is an understandable symbol of compassion.

Hope

As a noun, hope means optimism. As a verb, to hope is to actively believe that we will get what we need or strongly desire. We must all live in hope to some degree. But the gift of hope is more than this; it is a sense of deep trust in what is and what is to come. Like a rainbow in the sky after a rainstorm, this symbol reminds us to hope.

Joy

Joy is the sense of delight and well-being that we all have within us. We're readily aware of joy when we are laughing and having fun, but even in sad or challenging times, joy is available. We are more likely then to experience joy quietly and softly. Joy is always within us regardless of what is going on outside of us. The shining sun is a powerful symbol for joy. It is bright and delightful. Even when hidden by clouds, it's still there. Sometimes our own joy shines brightly, sometimes it does not, but it is always there.

Talent

The gift of talent includes many special abilities. Discovering what these are is one of our jobs in life. Another is to decide how we will develop our talent and abilities to make a difference in the world. What we enjoy doing gives us clues as to what our special abilities are. We discover them as we grow and develop. A tree is an apt symbol of talent. The trunk represents the overall gift of talent. The branches represent our many growing special abilities. A tree in bloom symbolizes that our special abilities are being used.

Imagination

Imagination is a powerful gift. We use it in many ways every day, like when we pretend, solve problems, create, and visualize. It also helps us cope with anxieties and challenges. Using our imaginations, we can explore our hopes, our dreams, and our lifelong goals. Every great achievement started as an idea—an idea within someone's imagination. Clouds are symbols of imagination because we often see images when we look at their shapes and movements.

Reverence

Children may or may not have heard this word. But like all the gifts, they know what it is and they have the capacity for it. Reverence is a sense of wonder and awe. It is a kind of deep respect and appreciation. When we feel reverence we might whisper, *"Wow."* Stars are symbols of reverence because they inspire wonder and awe.

Wisdom

Wisdom is similar to knowledge and comprehension, yet it is different. Wisdom offers us guidance and understanding of the truly important things in life. Wisdom helps us to make good choices. It's like an inner compass. Conscience is a part of wisdom. We are born with wisdom, and we learn how to listen to and better use it as we grow and age. Sometimes we gain wisdom by making mistakes and learning from them. An arrow is a symbol of wisdom because wisdom gives us direction and points the way.

Love

Love is related both to feelings and to actions. We can *feel* love for ourselves, for other people, for animals, for nature, for the Earth, for things, and for the Creator. We can *give* love, *show* love, and *receive* love. We can *be* love. It is healthy and important to love ourselves and take good care of ourselves. At times we may feel unloving or unlovable, but there are many things we can do to help us feel loving and lovable again. The heart is a well-known and universal symbol of love.

Faith

Everyone has faith. Faith is our capacity to believe with our minds and our hearts and to trust in what we cannot see. Faith is often associated with beliefs about the Divine. People of all cultures have beliefs about life, order in the universe, and how it is unfolding. It is important that we respect one another's cherished beliefs in this area. We can see evidence of the gift of faith in all people in other ways too. For example, we have faith that the earth is moving around the sun. We have faith that the sun will rise tomorrow. Every day we take actions and make choices that are influenced by what we believe and what we trust. Like all the gifts, faith is very powerful. The circle is a symbol of faith because it represents eternity. We can also see the circle as holding all the precious things in which we have faith.

Acknowledgments

With gratitude, I acknowledge the inspiration, guidance, and help that came in so many forms with each step of the writing and publication of each of The Twelve Gifts books and for every mile of The Polished Stone Tour. This new book reaches back and draws material from the making and marketing of all the previous ones.

To all the people I encountered in my journey: thank you for sharing your time, talents, help, beliefs, dreams, and stories. You have greatly enriched my life. I am sending you waves of love, gratitude, and blessings.

I want to name those whose personal stories are shared in this book. Thank you Mazi, Heather, Sharon, Jamie, the Shermans, Zoey, Penny, Olivia,

Jack, Margaret, Kathy, Nancy, Kay, Betsy, Leah and Ben, Keith, Alaina, Terri, Fred, Sheila, Michael, Granny, and Andrea. Some of the names in these stories have been changed. Thank you also to all who preferred to share without being identified, to all whose name I have forgotten, and to all whose name I never learned.

With deep appreciation, I also acknowledge John and Anna, Anna Victoria, Stephen Albert, Dr. Cavalcant, Etty Hillesum, Uncle Ray, Uncle Spike, Bob Brenly, Lance Armstrong, Father Mychal Judge, Arthur, and Mrs. Cougan.

I acknowledge all the schools, bookstores, shelters, centers for healing, libraries, hospitals, prisons, places of worship, and TV and radio stations that welcomed me.

I especially want to acknowledge all the teachers we met. I applaud you and thank you for the important work you do, day by day, educating our children and helping them to see their gifts. Thank you for welcoming me, too!

Acknowledgments

Thank you also, dear children, for listening, sharing, and being open to learning more about your gifts.

I thank all the media folks who gave coverage to The Twelve Gifts message.

A special thanks to all the stores—the chains, the independent bookstores, and the specialty retailers—who hosted me.

In addition to "thank you," I want to apologize for losing touch in some cases. I'm sorry for the letters and emails that I failed to respond to during the tour. I tried my best, and I know that some things slipped through cracks. Communication was among the greatest challenges on that trip.

In preparing *Touchstones* for publication, in addition to all those who shared stories, I thank those who helped me edit this book: Nancy, Willy, Stephanie, Francesca, and Doran.

Thank you, designers: Karen at Chalk Design and friends at 1106 Design.

For permission to quote your wise and beautiful words: Thank you, Mark Stanton Welch,

Jana Stanfield, Karen Taylor-Good, John Morton, Susan Kay Wyatt, Kasi Peters, and Rob Peters.

Thank you, friends, for supporting and encouraging me. Thank you, dear family, especially Frank, Stephanie, and Krista. A special thanks to Glenice, Karen Hope, Kathy, and Kyra.

Like raising a child, publishing a book takes a village. Thank you again to all who helped me "raise" this book.

Thank *you*, dear reader. Without you, there would be little reason to put The Twelve Gifts message in this form.

About Charlene

Charlene Gorda Costanzo is an award-winning author, workshop facilitator, wife, mother of two adult daughters, and grandmother of twins. She holds a B.A. in Philosophy from St. Bonaventure University and an M.A. in Spiritual Psychology from the University of Santa Monica.

Originally from New Jersey, she has resided in New York, Texas, Arizona, and Florida. During a one-year book tour to launch *The Twelve Gifts of Birth*, Charlene and her husband visited forty-nine states.

The Twelve Gifts series of fables began in 1987 when Charlene wrote *The Twelve Gifts of Birth* as a life message for her own, then teenage, daughters. Twelve years later she published the book and began presenting its message in schools, shelters, prisons, hospitals, and places of worship throughout the United States

The Twelve Gifts for Healing was written while Charlene was in treatment for advanced Non-Hodgkin's Lymphoma in 2001. "Cancer led me to examine my convictions and look at these life gifts more deeply. Truly, they helped me heal," she says.

The Twelve Gifts in Marriage comes from the ups and downs, ebbs and flows, and hurts and healings that are a part of every long-term relationship.

The Thirteenth Gift is a novella inspired by Charlene's deep appreciation for the gift of wonder and her life-long fascination with stones.

To learn more about The Twelve Gifts and to contact Charlene, please visit www.charlenecostanzo.com.

About FEATHERFEW, the Publisher

Featherfew is one of the many wildflowers that grow in wastelands and barren soil. Despite inhospitable conditions, they thrive along roadsides, in vacant lots, even through sidewalk cracks. Humbly, perennially, without comfort, fine breeding, or cultivation, they bring rich color, sweet fragrance, and simple beauty into the world. And, they bring healing. Featherfew, in particular, is known for calming distress and lifting low spirits.

Like tenacious wildflowers, the gifts of FEATHERFEW small press are designed to bring into the world a measure of healing and joy. FEATHERFEW shares in the vision of a world growing in peace with an appreciation of the dignity of all people and the goodness of all creation.

A portion of the profits is donated to The Twelve Gifts of Birth Foundation, which supports programs that prevent abuse and promote the well-being of children.

"And now, dear brothers and sisters, one final thing. Fix your thoughts on what is true, and honorable, and right, and pure, and lovely, and admirable. Think about things that are excellent and worthy of praise."

—Phil. 4:8